HOW THINGS WORK

DISCOVER SECRETS AND SCIENCE BEHIND BOUNCE HOUSES, HOVERCRAFT, ROBOTICS, AND EVERYTHING IN BETWEEN

T. J. RESLER

NATIONAL GEOGRAPHIC
WASHINGTON, D.C.

WHAT'S INSIDE

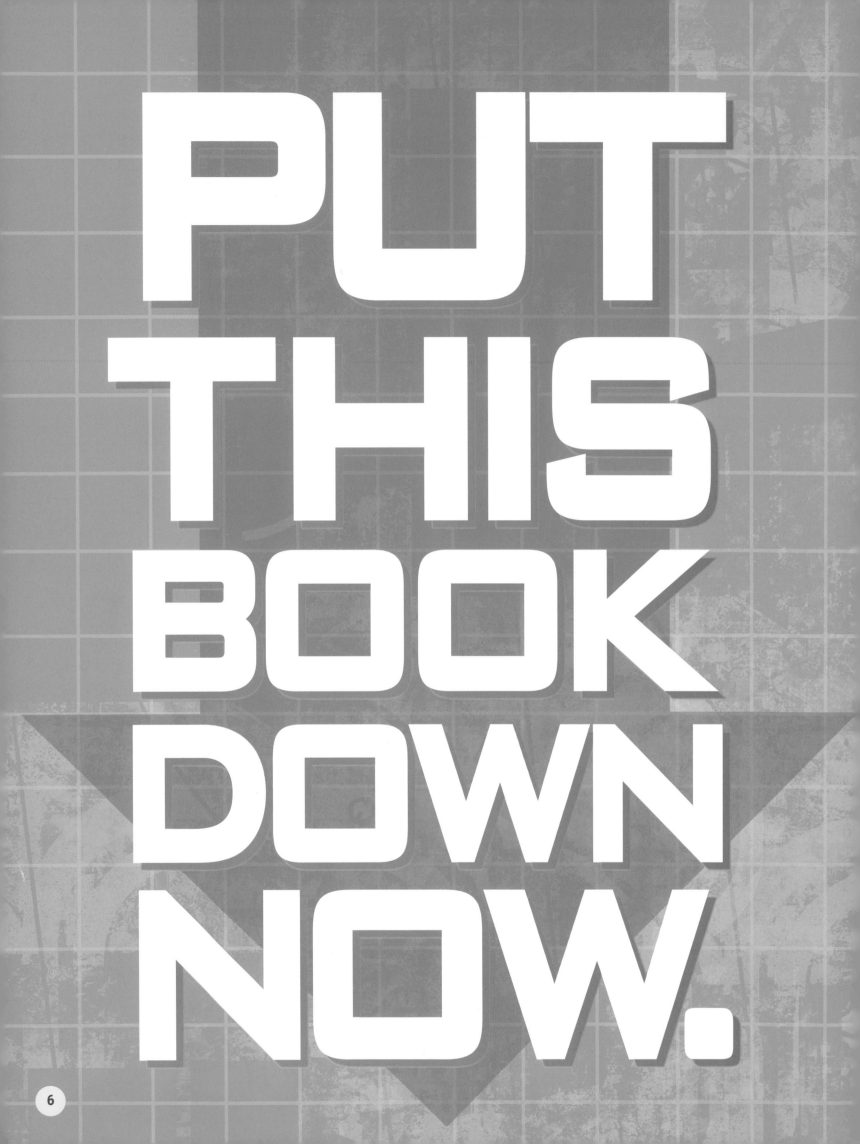

IT'S DANGEROUS. IT MIGHT MAKE YOU THINK YOU CAN DO IMPOSSIBLE THINGS.

Still reading? You must be one of those. The kind of kid who thinks "just because" isn't a real answer. The kid who says "Why not?" when you're told not to do something. You want to explore. You want to know *why* something works. You want to know *how*.

OK, dive in. But don't say we didn't warn you. This book is full of *why* and *how*. You'll discover science-fiction inventions that have become science fact. You'll unravel the mysteries behind the gadgets in your home that cook and clean for you. (No, not your parents.) You'll learn about things in your school that are much cooler than homework sheets. You'll find out *why* simulators feel so real and why you don't pop a bounce house when you jump in it. You'll be transported into a world of machines that zoom, fly, and dive.

HOW IT WORKS
If you need a quick answer about how something works, you'll find it on the "Just the Facts" page. If you want to dive in deeper, check out the "Tell Me More" section.

Along the way, you'll meet the real-life scientists, engineers, inventors, and innovators who push limits to make the next breakthrough. They're people willing to risk everything, and who refuse to believe "it can't be done."

They find mistakes fascinating. They solve the unsolvable. You'll also find out the weird and inspiring stories—the accidental discoveries, the "Eureka!" moments, the repeated failures—behind some inventions in "Tales from the Lab."

Oh, and you'll get your turn, too. Become a scientist or engineer and tackle the "Try This!" challenges. Experiment, invent, create, and explore. You just may find you can do something impossible.

> **"YOU MUST BE ONE OF THOSE. THE KIND OF KID WHO THINKS 'JUST BECAUSE' ISN'T A REAL ANSWER."**

EVER WONDERED HOW A MICROWAVE WORKS, ERASER MAKES MARKS DISAPPEAR, OR VERBIKE FLOATS?

answers to more complete explanations, we've got you covered. From making sense of sci-fi to surprising new discoveries about home, school, and being on the go, this book shows you the fascinating science of HOW THINGS WORK.

INCLUDES
- detailed diagrams and revealing photos
- fascinating info and incredible facts
- hands-on activities to get you involved
- inspiring bios of engineers, inventors, and scientists
- real-life stories of amazing inventions and unbelievable innovations

kids.nationalgeographic.com

REINFORCED LIBRARY BINDING

NATIONAL GEOGRAPHIC KIDS

HOW THINGS WORK

DISCOVER SECRETS AND SCIENCE BEHIND BOUNCE HOUSES, HOVERCRAFTS, ROBOTICS, AND EVERYTHING IN BETWEEN

Sit. Roll over. Good human!

T. J. RESLER

CHAPTER 1

Beam ME UP

COOL GADGETS AND SCIENTIFIC DISCOVERIES

don't just come from laboratories.
Many are dreamed up in the minds of storytellers.

Science fiction looks to the future, and for hundreds of years, it's asked "What if ... ?" Like, "What if we could fly?" or "What if we could build robots or make things disappear?" Sci-fi does more than just ask questions, though. It sparks imaginations. It inspires people to act. Some inventors read sci-fi. Then they ask, "Why *not* build a robot?" or they make a bionic arm. They figure out how to make something disappear. They invent, engineer, and discover. They turn science fiction into science fact.

SWEET RIDES

How do HOVERBIKES and HOVERBOARDS fly?

Check It Out!

Two awesome inventions promise science-fiction fans the rides of their lives. That's right—real hoverbikes and hoverboards. Don't expect to zip through forests as fast as a *Star Wars* speeder bike, or to outdistance a bunch of bullies like in *Back to the Future*. But these real hovercraft will offer a ride that's unlike any other in this world. Climb on board to check out these sweet rides.

What makes hovercraft float ?

How do the hoverbike and the hoverboard move ?

Where can they go ?

JUST THE FACTS

How Do Hovercraft Float on Air?

Hovercraft glide along on a cushion of air. They create the air cushion with powerful fans, or propellers, that push air down toward the ground, creating the lift that makes the vehicle hover. Hovercraft are specially designed to trap most of the air underneath them. Depending on the strength of their engines, they can float anywhere from a few inches (centimeters) to 10 feet (3 m) off the ground. To move, hovercraft create more air currents to push them forward. They can create an air cushion on any smooth surface. Hovercraft are more common on waterways, but the hoverbike glides over land or water. The hoverboard needs a special surface to do its tricks.

Unlike some "hoverboards" which have wheels, the **HENDO BOARD** actually hovers.

Bike ...

Several inventors are working on hoverbikes. One being developed, the Aero-X, zips over flat ground, hills, and water. It's about the size of a car but rides like a motorcycle, only in the air. Its riders guide it by moving its grips in the direction they want to go. This hoverbike goes up to 45 miles an hour (72 km/h) and can hover up to 12 feet (3.7 m) in the air, but its inventors think riders will feel most comfortable at about half that height. The craft is powered by two large fans, or propellers, lined up one in front of another. It'll run 1 hour and 15 minutes on a tank of gasoline.

... Versus Board

The hoverboard model made by Hendo uses a different technology from most hovercraft. The board has four small, disc-shaped magnets that are electrically charged. The designers call these magnets "hover engines," because they create a strong magnetic field with the surface below. The magnetic field lifts the board about an inch (2.5 cm) off the ground. Hoverboards need to float above a special surface that interacts with the magnets, and so they require special "hoverparks" with ramps, bowls, and half-pipes for tricks. Riders provide a push to get the board moving.

ARE WE **THERE** YET?

Plenty of storytellers agreed that **hovercraft would exist one day.** But it seems they couldn't agree on when that day would come. Check out this timeline of **fictional hovercraft,** and find out when writers predicted we'd be able to take our hoverbikes out for a spin. (Hint: Real life is a little bit behind schedule!)

A LONG TIME AGO

In 1983's *Star Wars Episode VI: Return of the Jedi*, writer and director George Lucas imagined speeder bikes—small, agile hovercraft.

FUN FACT

FRANCE EXPERIMENTED WITH **A HIGH-SPEED HOVERTRAIN,** THE AEROTRAIN, BETWEEN 1965 AND 1977 BUT DECIDED INSTEAD TO DEVELOP **THE HIGH-SPEED ELECTRIC TGV** (TRAIN À GRANDE VITESSE).

HOVERBOARD

It's a smooth ride on this board.

In 2014, a video showing professional skateboarder **TONY HAWK** and other celebrities riding a "HUVr" hoverboard went viral on the Internet. It turned out to be a prank.

The idea of riding on an air cushion isn't new. British shipbuilder John Thornycroft got a patent for an **AIR-CUSHION SHIP** in the 1870s, but the right kind of engines to make it work weren't available at the time.

HOVERBIKE

It's not a *Star Wars* speeder bike, but it's got plenty of awesome.

ELECTRICALLY CHARGED MAGNETS

FANS (PROPELLERS)

1726
When Jonathan Swift wrote his classic book *Gulliver's Travels*, he dreamed up Laputa, a floating island controlled by magnetic levitation.

2015
When Marty McFly time-travels to 2015 in the 1989 comedy *Back to the Future Part II*, hoverboards are all the rage.

2062
The Jetsons, first aired in 1962, predicts a future where flying cars, robot maids, and hoverboards are commonplace!

FUN FACT

BRITISH ENGINEER CHRISTOPHER COCKERELL, **WHO INVENTED THE HOVERCRAFT** IN THE MID-1950s, WAS KNIGHTED FOR HIS CONTRIBUTIONS TO ENGINEERING. CALL HIM "SIR CHRISTOPHER."

WANT TO **KNOW MORE?**

TELL ME MORE

SMOOTH RIDES

Hovercraft provide smooth rides even when they're traveling over rough ground. Why? The answer is in the air cushion. It reduces friction, which happens when two things rub against each other. The more friction, the harder it is for something to move. Wheels moving on a road or over dirt create more friction than a hovercraft moving over air does.

MAGNETIC MAGIC

When two magnets are near each other, there's a magnetic field between them—an area where they try to pull together or push apart.

With some magnets, called electromagnets, you can control when they have a magnetic field.

Electromagnets need a jolt of energy to get their charge. (Other magnets, called permanent magnets, are—you guessed it—magnetic all the time.) Hendo designers use these forces to make their board hover. They combined the board's magnetic fields in a way (exactly how is a secret) that makes them stronger and more focused. When the board's magnets get near a special coating on the floor, it creates an electromagnetic field that pushes the board's magnets away.

Sir Christopher Cockerell shows off a hovercraft he designed.

TRY THIS!

Have you ever noticed how magnets sometimes snap together, but other times they push themselves apart or to the side? All magnets have two opposite poles, north and south. When you line up two magnets so their opposite poles are closest to each other (north and south), they attract each other and try to pull together, even if they aren't right next to each other. But if you try to put the same poles next to each other (north and north, for example), the magnets repel or push away from each other. Grab a couple of powerful magnets and check it out yourself.

FUN FACTS

● In 1716, Swedish philosopher and designer Emanuel Swedenborg designed **a flying saucer**-shaped aircraft that would travel over water on an air cushion. It would have required the pilot to use **oarlike scoops** to push air under it.

● Once **Christopher Cockerell** figured out how to make a hovercraft work in **1955,** he built a model out of a cat food can, a coffee can, and some kitchen scales.

Cockerell's hovercraft, which carries three people, crosses the English Channel.

● **The first hovercraft race was** in 1964 in Canberra, Australia. Eleven hovercraft, built by people in their backyards, entered the race. Two had technical difficulties, another **sank,** and three had to be towed to shore.

RIDING ON AIR

See how the hoverbike gets a boost.

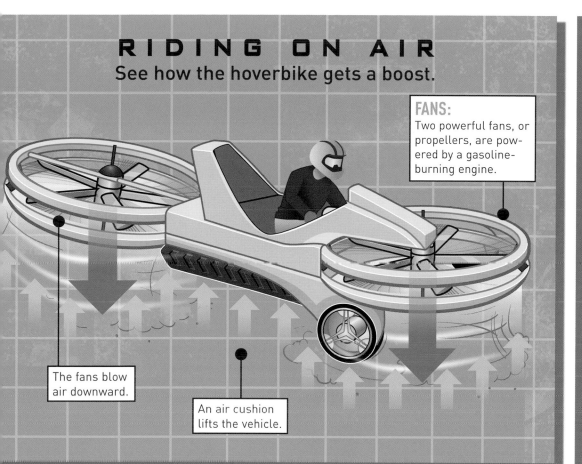

FANS:
Two powerful fans, or propellers, are powered by a gasoline-burning engine.

The fans blow air downward.

An air cushion lifts the vehicle.

GETTING A LIFT

Check out how repulsive magnets can make an attractive ride.

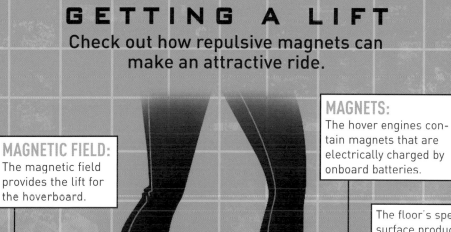

MAGNETIC FIELD:
The magnetic field provides the lift for the hoverboard.

MAGNETS:
The hover engines contain magnets that are electrically charged by onboard batteries.

The floor's special surface produces a magnetic field, which pushes the hoverboard's magnets up and away.

Myth vs. FACT

MYTH: You can soar high above the rooftops in your very own hovercraft.

FACT: In 1957, *Popular Mechanics* showed us a personal hovercraft—what it called a "flying-fan vehicle"—that we'd be able to buy for the "price of a good car." The magazine explained that a ducted fan would boost the vehicle, but it showed the hovercar flying above rooftops. Oops! Hovercraft can't fly that high. They'd be too far from the ground they need to push off of. Inventor William "Doc" Bertelsen proved that fact in 1959 by building a real hovercar. To get into the wild blue yonder, recent inventors have designed car-airplane combos. But, so far, those vehicles have been too expensive and use too much fuel. It's been tough to make flying vehicles that are easy to control, safe, and quiet enough to use where a lot of people live. But inventors are determined to solve those problems. Then we just have to figure out how to get stoplights in the sky.

POPULAR MECHANICS MAGAZINE

WRITTEN SO YOU CAN UNDERSTAND IT

HILLER'S AERIAL SEDAN
—your flying car for 1967—page 74
Stand by for Satellite Take-Off!
Owners Report: OLDSMOBILE
HOW TO OUTSMART HOUSEBREAKERS

WORLD AT YOUR FINGERTIPS

How do TABLETS know so much?

Check It Out!

Prepare to time travel. It's 1968. When people hear the word "computer," they picture a room filled with whirring machines the size of refrigerators. *The first desktop computers won't appear in homes for another decade.* So when moviegoers watch the futuristic *2001: A Space Odyssey* and see astronauts watching a news program on a thin computerized tablet ... Mind. Blown.

How does a tablet find all the information I look up?

What's the difference between a tablet and a computer?

How does the tablet know which way I'm holding it?

You mean this can do more than take super-size selfies?

JUST THE FACTS

How Can Something So Small Do So Much?

Thanks to miniature electronics and cloud computing, you can have instant access from wherever you are to an entire library of books, games, art supplies, knowledge, and people. One of the awesome devices that lets you do all this is your tablet, a small computer you operate by touch. Using it is easy. You press a button to turn it on or wake it up. You tap an app on the screen to begin doing what you want—maybe drawing a picture or listening to music. The app opens a program that's either on your tablet or on the Internet. Most apps have a menu of different things you can do. So if you start the email app, you can either read the messages you received or start writing a message to someone else. After you write the message, another tap on the screen sends it on its way. It travels over the Internet and lands in your friend's email inbox—usually in an instant.

What's an App?

An application, or app, is a small, specialized program that tells your tablet how to do what you want it to do. Some popular apps let you send email, browse the Web, listen to music, and keep track of your activities on a calendar. If you want to play a game, learn Spanish, or find out the time in Russia, you can use an app for that. Pretty much anything you want to do—or maybe don't want to do—has an app. There are games for cats and whistles for dogs, an app that makes your screen looked cracked, and another that repeats everything you say in a funny voice. You can use apps to see how you'd look with a mustache or to tell someone "moo" (that's it—just "moo"). There's even an app for hunting ghosts!

Touch screens need to pick up the electrical charge from your **FINGERS**—which can be a problem if you're wearing gloves in the winter, or if you're in the bath. One British designer created the **FINGER-NOSE STYLUS** for when you need an extra hand.

Why can't you use a regular pen or pencil to work your touch screen? Most touch screens need to **SENSE AN ELECTRICAL CHARGE.** Plastic and wood are insulators, so electricity cannot flow through them.

CHARGED UP

The human body has **an electrical charge.** This electricity allows your brain to get signals to and from the rest of your body, which then lets you do all kinds of awesome things. Still, humans don't generate much electrical charge, at least not compared to these other electrifying objects.

Human body
10 to 100 millivolts

Electric eel
600 volts

Lightning
up to 1 billion volts

Car battery
12.6 volts

TOUCHY  SUBJECT

Touching a screen is a handy way to control a tablet. But how can a tablet understand what you're tapping and swiping with your fingers?

kids.nationalgeographic.com

WHICH SHARK ARE YOU?

APP:
A specialized program that lets you do all kinds of cool things, like send messages, get online, or discover your inner shark.

Long before *2001: A Space Odyssey* and *Star Trek*, writer E. M. Forster envisioned a type of tablet. In his 1909 science-fiction story **"THE MACHINE STOPS,"** people communicated through handheld round plates, a type of live video call.

SHOCKING?

Tablets read your touches by sensing electrical charges. No shocks involved.

A touch screen has several layers of special glass sandwiched together in a way that stores an electrical charge. The top and bottom layers of glass are made so electricity can flow through them easily.

Anyone who's gotten a little shock from touching a friend or car door in the winter knows that electricity can flow through us. When we touch the screen, we change the electrical field of the screen. The tablet senses the change and knows what we're telling it to do.

The middle layer is an insulator, meaning it does not let electricity flow very well. It makes sure the electrical charges in the screen wait for your touch.

WANT TO KNOW MORE?

TELL ME MORE

WHAT MAKES A TABLET DO YOUR BIDDING?

A tablet looks pretty simple from the outside, but it's hiding a lot of advanced technology inside. The guts of a tablet are similar to what you'd find in a larger computer, only much smaller and packed in more tightly. Most tablets aren't as strong as larger computers—and that's a good thing. Many computers work so hard that they generate a lot of heat. They need fans inside to cool them. Tablets don't have room for internal fans, so it's helpful that their computing parts don't work so hard. The same goes for tablet apps. They tend to be smaller and simpler than the programs on larger computers.

WEBS AND NETS AND CLOUDS—OH, MY!

When you turn on a tablet, are you connecting to the Internet, the Cloud, the World Wide Web, or what? Let's sort it out. The Internet is a worldwide network of computers linked together. They're real machines that you could touch. Most people imagine the Internet as a bunch of computers "somewhere out there." They could be floating up in the air for all we know! Actually, they couldn't, but that's probably why people started thinking of the Internet as "the Cloud." Same thing. The World Wide Web—also known as WWW or "the Web"—is different. It's the

information you can find on the Internet. It's organized in websites, like the pages that come up in a search. Just like the threads on a spiderweb, websites are connected by links. If you click or tap on a link, you'll open another website. You can become an instant expert.

TRY THIS!

Turn on a faucet to get a very narrow stream of water. Comb your (dry) hair several times—like a dozen times—with a plastic comb. (Or you can rub an inflated balloon on your hair.) Slowly move the comb (or balloon) toward the side of the water stream, without touching the water, and watch what happens. Do you see the water bend toward the comb? Your hair charged your comb with static electricity. Electrical charges in the comb and water interact—kind of like the way your finger interacts with the electrical field of a tablet's touch screen.

● Real computer tablets didn't exist when the **TV series Star Trek: The Next Generation** was filmed. The PADD (Personal Access Display Device) tablets used by the *Enterprise*'s crew were props.

● The first PADDs were made of **light boxes** covered with **transparent colored sheets.** Later, the series used video panels or added animation after shooting the scenes.

Dr. Phlox uses a tablet on *Star Trek: Enterprise.*

hardware + software

● Apps and programs are called **software.** The physical parts that make up your tablet are called **hardware.**

FUN FACTS

MICRO MARVEL

The inside of a tablet is a feat of engineering genius. Let's see why.

WI-FI & GPS:
Special parts connect your tablet to the Internet wirelessly and, if you want, let satellites know where you are so you can find places nearby.

CAMERA:
Many tablets have a camera. The lens is often at the top of the tablet.

DISPLAY:
Displays can range from simple black and white to stunning full color.

CPU:
The "brain" of the tablet is called a microprocessor or central processing unit (CPU). It's a complete computation engine on a chip smaller than a dime.

ENCLOSURE/CASE:
The parts, or components, of a tablet are packed inside a case that can be made of either plastic or lightweight metal.

TOUCH SCREEN:
Topped by strong, scratch-resistant glass or plastic, the touch screen relays our commands to the tablet's computer processor.

SPEAKERS:
Small speakers play music and other sounds.

SENSORS:
Tablets contain several sensors. Some of them tell the display when to get brighter or dimmer. Others figure out how you're holding the tablet, so the screen flips.

CONNECTORS/PORTS:
Special connectors called ports let you plug in other things, like a charger.

BATTERY PACK:
A rechargeable battery pack supplies the power.

The REAL DEAL

Sci-fi gadgets usually are much cooler than the real things they inspire. But when it comes to tablet computers, it's tough to pick a winner. In many ways, real tablets do more than their sci-fi inspiration. The earliest tablet, a handheld round plate in E. M. Forster's 1909 science-fiction story "The Machine Stops," let people communicate through a live video call. But if they wanted to send a written message, they couldn't do it on the tablets. They had to write down the message and send it through a tube delivery system. Even the amazing News Pad tablets from Arthur C. Clarke's 1968 story *2001: A Space Odyssey* only allowed people to watch television and read newspapers. *Star Trek*'s earliest tablets were little more than electronic clipboards, though the series eventually gave the thin, handheld devices the power to run the entire starship. Before we declare real tablets the winner, though, consider this: The News Pad pulled up information from any newspaper on Earth in only a few milliseconds from far out in space, while the ship was speeding away from Earth at thousands of miles (or kilometers) an hour. See if you can find anyone who's ever gotten that kind of Wi-Fi connection.

2001: A Space Odyssey

Think about all the people using tablets at this very second. Many are sending email, others are surfing the Web, and some are downloading books or watching movies. All that information travels on radio waves. Why isn't it getting all jumbled up?

If all that info tried to ride the same wave, it'd create an epic traffic jam. Lucky for us, someone figured out how to spread our email

> ## "WHO WAS THAT GENIUS? A MOVIE STAR."

and Web searches over the entire spectrum of radio waves. Who was this genius? A computer scientist working in a high-tech lab? Nope. It was a movie star.

The star was Hedy Lamarr, a glamorous actress in the late 1930s through the 1950s. She was born in Austria in 1914, but she moved to Hollywood when she was 22 years old to be in movies.

She was already a star when, in 1940, Nazi German submarines torpedoed British ships carrying innocent people fleeing World War II. Hedy was horrified. She wanted to help. But what could a movie star do? It turns out, quite a lot.

She invented a secret way to guide torpedoes using radio waves. Easy peasy, right?

THE RIGHT STUFF

Hedy had always been interested in how things worked. When she wasn't making movies, she was inventing.

She also knew about radio-controlled weapons. In

Hedy Lamarr

Austria, she'd been married to a rich weapons maker. He invited his customers, including German admirals and generals, to dinner parties. He expected his wife to play the charming hostess, just smiling and looking pretty.

No one realized that Hedy was learning all their technical secrets.

From those dinner party conversations, she knew the challenges affecting radio-controlled weapons. To help the United States and its allies, she'd have to make it impossible for the Nazis to jam or interfere with the radio signals guiding the torpedoes. But how?

JUMPING AHEAD

Hedy may have gotten an idea from a game she played in Hollywood with her friend George Antheil, a music composer. One of them would start playing a song on the piano, and the other would have to follow along. Their hands would hop all over the keyboard as they tried to stay together.

That was it! If the radio signal hopped from one radio wave to another, the Nazis wouldn't detect it. A secret code would tell both the transmitter, which sends out the radio signal, and the torpedo's receiver when and where to hop.

George figured they could punch the secret code onto special ribbons like he used for a player piano. Then the torpedo would know when to hop to a different radio wave, and it would be guided to its target. Hedy and George got a patent for their invention in 1942.

Their "Secret Communication" system showed how to spread information over the entire spectrum of radio waves. Other people built on their ideas, and now our email, downloads, books, and movies can travel on radio waves without getting in each other's way.

George Antheil

HEDY **INVENTED A CUBE** THAT, WHEN PUT IN WATER, WOULD CREATE A **SOFT DRINK,** BUT NOT EVEN HEDY LIKED THE **TASTE OF IT.**

BORN **HEDWIG EVA MARIA KIESLER,** HEDY AGREED TO CHANGE HER NAME TO SOUND **MORE HOLLYWOOD.**

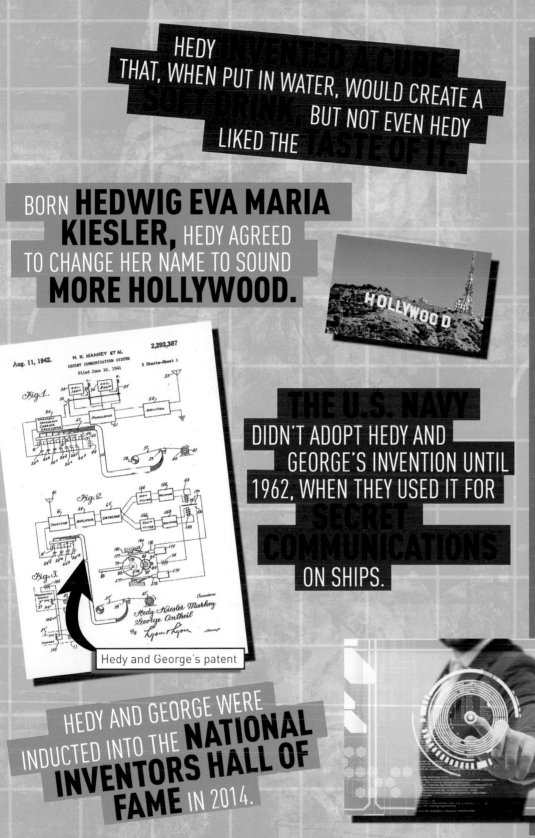

Hedy and George's patent

THE U.S. NAVY DIDN'T ADOPT HEDY AND GEORGE'S INVENTION UNTIL 1962, WHEN THEY USED IT FOR **SECRET COMMUNICATIONS** ON SHIPS.

HEDY AND GEORGE WERE INDUCTED INTO THE **NATIONAL INVENTORS HALL OF FAME** IN 2014.

Make It BETTER!

People have always had all kinds of ideas about what the future of technology and communication would look like. For some people of the past, that future is today. Of course, we're not chatting with aliens or driving flying cars yet. But for all the things they got wrong about the future, they did get some things right. For example, the characters in *The Jetsons* cartoon could video chat, and *Star Trek* predicted flip phones (which have already been replaced with the smartphones we know and love).

Wireless communication is something we use every day in the 21st century. We've got all kinds of ways to talk to one another—cell phones, text, email, video ... the list goes on and on. Now it's your turn to design the wireless communication of the future. How do you think people will be getting in touch in the year 2100? What about the year 3000?

THE WAY OF WAVES

We can't see them, but there are thousands of **radio waves flying through the air around us.** They all travel at the same speed, but some are shorter and go up and down more times than the longer waves. The number of times a wave moves up and down in a second is called its frequency. All together, the radio waves make up a "spectrum," the entire range of different frequencies.

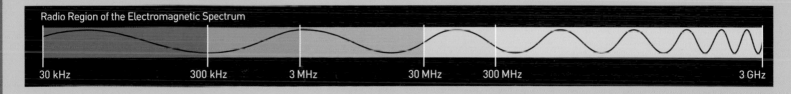

Radio Region of the Electromagnetic Spectrum

| 30 kHz | 300 kHz | 3 MHz | 30 MHz | 300 MHz | 3 GHz |

NOW YOU SEE ME ...

How does an INVISIBILITY CLOAK make something vanish?

Check It Out!

It's the ultimate way to hide: an invisibility cloak. It helped Harry Potter escape a lot of close calls, and it let the Romulans slip away from *Star Trek's Enterprise*. Are invisibility cloaks only found in fiction? Not anymore. Scientists have made an invisibility cloak that's so simple any muggle could use it. Well, maybe not Dudley Dursley. For the rest of you, get ready to see how things can disappear from sight.

How big of a thing can it hide?

Can it make a person invisible?

How do I wear it?

JUST THE FACTS

Out of Sight

Want to know how an invisibility cloak makes things vanish? Well, it doesn't. It makes them vanish from sight. They're still there. We just can't see them. In other words, cloaking is an optical illusion. Researchers at the University of Rochester, in New York, figured out a simple way to pull off this illusion by using four lenses. When the lenses are lined up in a precise way, they bend light around an object that's between them. The light passes right on by as if the object isn't even there. And to our eyes, it isn't. Instant invisibility—no cloak required.

If It's Not a Cape, What's It Good For?

Scientists around the world have been working on cloaking technology. (So far, no one has come up with an invisibility cloak like Harry's.) Many of the ideas work only in laboratories with complicated equipment or super expensive materials. The Rochester cloak doesn't cost much—less than $100 for a simple version—and is easy to build. The size of what it can cloak is only limited by the size of its lenses. Could it cloak starships and wizards? Doubtful. It takes a while to set up, but it might have other uses. It could be mounted on trucks or cars to cloak the window frames that normally block part of the driver's view of the road. Surgeons could cloak their hands to better see what they're operating on. That would be worth seeing.

We may not be able to cloak a starship, but stealth aircraft have some neat tricks to avoid detection. They use **RADAR-ABSORBING DARK PAINT,** optical camouflage, and other techniques to sneak by unnoticed.

REFRACTION IN ACTION

Refraction happens when light enters something that changes its speed, bending the light. Have you ever seen white light go through a prism? **What comes out is a rainbow.** That's refraction. All the colors that make up white light bend differently in the prism, making it easy to see them once they come out the other side. Violet light bends the most, and red bends the least.

THE LIGHT ALWAYS BENDS IN THIS ORDER, FROM LEAST TO MOST:

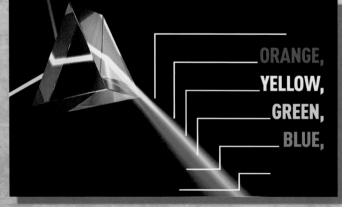

ORANGE,
YELLOW,
GREEN,
BLUE,

FUN FACT

LONG BEFORE HARRY POTTER, AMERICAN SCIENCE-FICTION WRITER RAY CUMMINGS INCLUDED AN **"INVISIBLE CLOAK"** IN HIS 1930 NOVEL *BRIGANDS OF THE MOON*. HIS CLOAK WAS POWERED BY ELECTRONICS.

SORRY, [👀] SIGHT

The lenses in the Rochester cloak bend light around the object instead of letting the light bounce off of it. Without light rays reflecting off the object and into our eyes, we can't see it. Check out how the Rochester cloak plays with light.

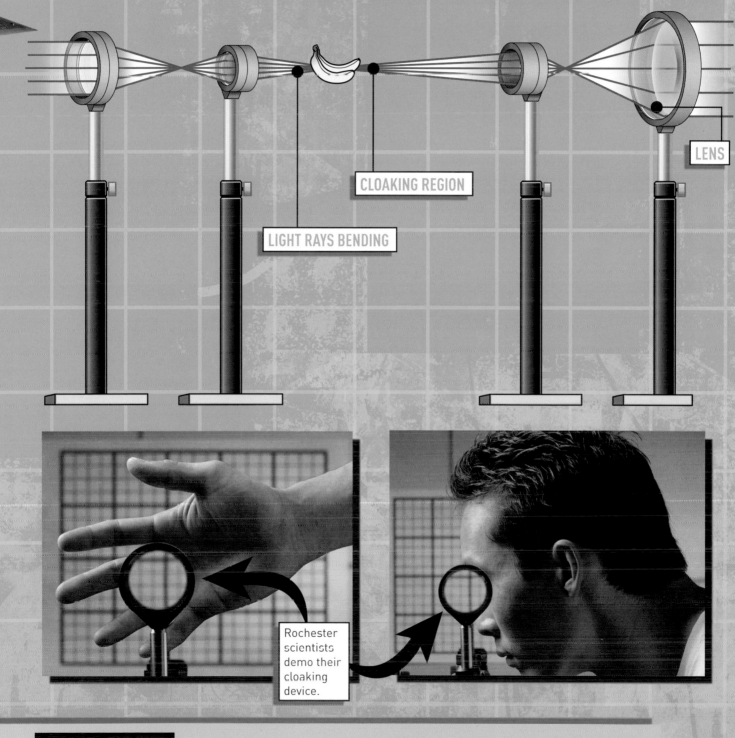

CLOAKING REGION

LIGHT RAYS BENDING

LENS

Rochester scientists demo their cloaking device.

FUN FACT ————————————————

STAR TREK HAD **A STARSHIP** THAT CLOAKED ITSELF IN A 1966 EPISODE, BUT THE SHOW DIDN'T USE THE TERM **"CLOAKING DEVICE"** UNTIL TWO YEARS LATER.

WANT TO KNOW MORE?

TELL ME MORE

Why does bending light around an object make it invisible? The answer is in how our eyes work. The only way we can see things is if light bounces off them and enters our eyes. Each part of our eye is designed to work with light. The eye's colored part, the iris, opens and closes to control how much light gets in. The lens changes shape to focus the light rays on the back of the eye, where tiny light-sensing nerve cells convert them into electrical signals to send to our brain. If light doesn't get into our eye, the system doesn't work. If that happens, we can't see what's right in front of us.

BENDING LIGHT
The science behind the invisibility cloak is not alien to us. If you wear glasses, you already know a bit about bending light. To have perfect vision, light rays entering the eye need to focus at the retina, the tissue at the back of the eye. For people without perfect vision, the lenses in glasses or contacts bend the light rays so they hit the right spot.

the Rochester cloaking device in action

TRY THIS!
Want to bend some light? Stick a pencil in a glass half-filled with water and look at it from the side. What happens to the pencil? Does it look bent or broken? It's not the pencil that's changed, of course. It's the light. The water is bending it. That's what happens to light when it passes from one medium to another. The same thing would happen with anything you put in the water, but the pencil trick is a classic.

● **Welsh mythology** dating back to the 12th century describes a **"mantle of invisibility"** that was one of King Arthur's most prized **possessions.**

FUN FACTS

● In 2012, Mercedes-Benz created an **"invisible car."** It actually used cameras to **beam images** of the background onto the car's surface. It was a promotional stunt.

● Rumor has it that in **1943 the U.S. Navy** made a ship invisible ("cloaked") to enemy devices, called the **Philadelphia Experiment,** after the place it supposedly occurred. The story is widely understood to be a **hoax** and **is completely untrue.** But many people still believe it.

Nothing to see here!

MASTER OF ILLUSION

To truly pull off the illusion of cloaking, the device can't mess up—or distort—how the background looks. See how the Rochester cloak covers up its trick by teaming up its lenses.

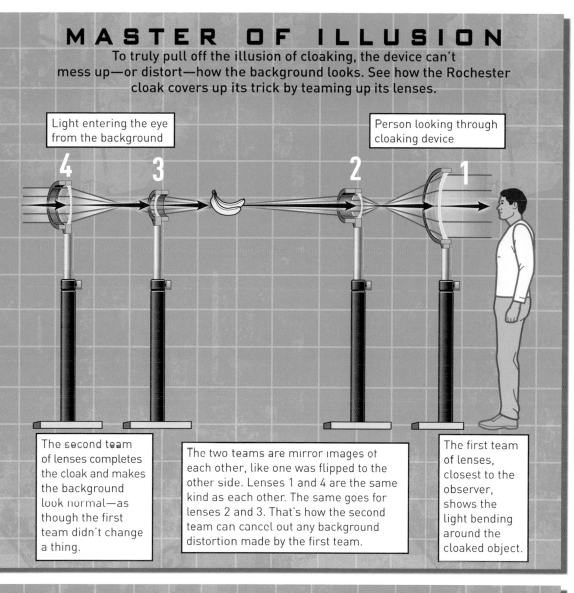

Light entering the eye from the background

Person looking through cloaking device

4　3　2　1

The second team of lenses completes the cloak and makes the background look normal—as though the first team didn't change a thing.

The two teams are mirror images of each other, like one was flipped to the other side. Lenses 1 and 4 are the same kind as each other. The same goes for lenses 2 and 3. That's how the second team can cancel out any background distortion made by the first team.

The first team of lenses, closest to the observer, shows the light bending around the cloaked object.

SYSTEMATIC DECEPTION

The Rochester cloaking device is a system. All four of its lenses work together to bend light rays in a way that tricks your eyes. If you wear glasses, you have your own lens system—though it helps you see more, not less! In your system, your glasses' lens helps the lens in your eye focus light rays at the retina, the tissue at the back of your eye, so that you have 20/20 vision. Take a look at how your system works.

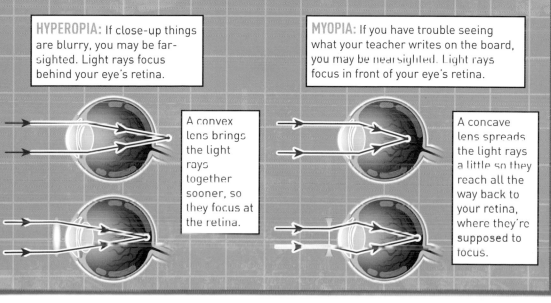

HYPEROPIA: If close-up things are blurry, you may be far-sighted. Light rays focus behind your eye's retina.

MYOPIA: If you have trouble seeing what your teacher writes on the board, you may be nearsighted. Light rays focus in front of your eye's retina.

A convex lens brings the light rays together sooner, so they focus at the retina.

A concave lens spreads the light rays a little so they reach all the way back to your retina, where they're supposed to focus.

The REAL DEAL

Yeah, we know. What you really, really want is a Harry Potter–style cape. Is it only a dream? Good news, would-be wizards and witches! Scientists are engineering special materials, called metamaterials, that can trick light. Like the invisibility cloak that uses lenses, these metamaterials make light rays bend around an object and come back together on its other side, as if the object isn't there at all. Here's how it works: The metamaterials contain pieces of precious metals, like gold and silver, 10,000 times smaller than grains of sand. Scientists can tinker with these tiny pieces to control the light rays. But don't hold your breath. A cape that makes you invisible is still decades away, and it's not going to be as good as Harry's. With all those precious metals, it's going to be thick, heavy, and really expensive. The biggest problem is that you won't be able to see through it. It may be a good hiding place, but don't try to sneak around.

Harry Potter's invisibility cloak got him out of lots of trouble.

BODY BUILDERS

How do BIONIC ARMS and LEGS move?

Check It Out!

Forget a pirate's hook. Modern, amazing bionic arms and legs like Luke Skywalker's high-tech limb aren't just found in a galaxy far, far away. Biomedical engineers are helping people who have lost limbs regain the ability to hold hands, play with toys, dance, and run again. Find out how machines can become extensions of our selves.

How are bionic limbs controlled?

Can bionic hands feel what they touch?

Is a bionic leg super-strong?

JUST THE FACTS

How Do Bionic Arms Reach Out?

Bionic limbs function almost like natural human limbs. They use robotic parts to replace missing flesh and bone. Your brain controls them by sending signals down nerves to special electrodes, little devices that pick up electrical signals. The electrodes either sit on your skin or are put inside your muscle or brain. A small computer inside the device turns your brain signals into actions. It also gathers information from sensors in the bionic limb and sends it back to your brain. A really advanced bionic arm has a hundred sensors. Some tell how the arm's joints are moving. Others measure how hard the fingertips are gripping and provide information about what they're touching.

Limited Limbs

Until recently, artificial body parts, called prostheses, weren't very effective. Sure, they were the right shape, the color of flesh, and not made of wood. But they didn't do much. A leg could bend; a hand could open and close like a crab's claw. But put a coin in a vending machine and unwrap a snack? Really hard. Many prosthetic hands use a harness-and-cable system designed in the 1800s and early 1900s. By scrunching a shoulder, you can open and close a mechanical hand. Even most motorized hands, around since the 1960s, aren't up to working vending machines. They grip more ways, but they don't feel natural. It takes a lot of practice and concentration just to hold an egg without crushing it.

KEEPING IN TOUCH

Get a grip on how advanced bionic arms, like the Modular Prosthetic Limb, can do almost everything a natural arm can.

JOINTS:
The Modular Prosthetic Limb has 26 joints, so it can move like a natural human arm. Traditional motorized arm prostheses only move two or three different ways.

MOTORS:
Inside the bionic arm are 17 motors that move the arm in a natural way.

SENSORS:
A person controls the arm through thought. The brain sends signals along nerves to electrodes, which communicate the brain's commands to the arm. Sensors gather information about how the arm is moving and send it back to the brain.

ATTACHMENT:
A custom-made body attachment holds the arm so it can move freely, carry weight, and connect to nerves remaining in the person's muscle.

t may not be long before bionics help make us faster and stronger. Researchers are working on bionic "exoskeletons," support structures that can attach to your body or legs. The bionics would make it easier for you to walk or run long distances or carry heavy loads. One researcher imagines a day when bionic legs could help you run 60 miles (96 km) over rough terrain without even breathing hard!

FEELINGS

The advanced technology of the Modular Prosthetic Limb lets a person feel and handle things just as someone with a natural hand would.

Several types of sensors send feedback to the brain. They tell it how the hand and fingers are moving and what they're touching.

A small computer inside the bionic hand translates the brain's commands into action.

A test pilot tries out a bionic exo-skeleton suit.

TRY THIS!

The simplest prosthetic arms have mechanical hands that only open and close. It's hard to imagine what it'd be like to have to rely on those, but you can get a bit of an idea with a simple experiment. Put on a thick glove like an oven mitt and grab a pair of tongs, the kitchen gadget you use to scoop up salad. Try to tie your shoes, crack an egg, or pick up a coin. Not so easy, right? That's why bio-medical engineers are working hard to develop artificial hands that feel and work like a natural hand.

● An ancient **Roman general,** Marcus Sergius, lost his right hand in the Second Punic War, 218-201 B.C. He had an **iron replacement** made so he could hold a shield and return to battle.

● The **earliest** known prosthesis dates back to **950–710** B.C. It is a toe **made of wood** and **leather** found on the mummy of an ancient Egyptian noblewoman.

FUN FACTS

PROFILE: David Moinina Sengeh

INNOVATOR, MENTOR, RISK TAKER

David Moinina Sengeh is from Sierra Leone, a small country in West Africa. And he's making a big impact around the world. He's been called a smart and daring innovator, someone who will shape the future.

David has figured out how to make artificial limbs fit better. He's inspired and mentored dozens of young innovators in Africa. He's won awards, been interviewed by magazines and TV programs, and given speeches around

> ## "FAILING IS PART OF THE PROCESS OF DEVELOPMENT."

the world. And he's done it all before finishing his graduate degree.

The secret to his success? He's not afraid to fail.

"Failing is part of the process of development," he says. He speaks from experience.

TRY, TRY AGAIN

David designed a better way to make prosthetic sockets, which are the parts that hold artificial limbs, or prostheses, onto people's bodies. A lot of prostheses hurt, so people stop wearing them. David saw that problem in his home country of Sierra Leone, where many people had lost arms and legs in a

decade-long war while he was growing up.

David wanted to change that. He started designing sockets on a computer. He used a special medical scanner to get the exact shape of a patient's body, and he 3-D-printed a perfect-fitting socket. He made it with several kinds of materials, so that it would be softer in some places and more supportive in others.

A war veteran who had tried dozens of different prostheses tested David's design for a leg and was amazed. He told David, "It's so soft, it's like walking on pillows."

But it wasn't easy creating the perfect design. It took a lot of experiments—and almost all of them failed at first. "But to me they are not failures," David says. "They are opportunities to do better and come up with smarter solutions."

INSPIRATION

David grew up willing to take risks and learn from them. He explored and pushed boundaries. He wanted to know about everything. When he was nine or ten years old, he watched his uncle, a surgeon, perform operations.

People need to be curious and willing to take risks, David says. "With passion, people can often do the impossible."

He started a program, Innovate Salone, to empower Kenyan, South African, and Sierra Leonian youth to identify challenges in their communities and figure out their own solutions.

"The creative thinking, the ability to dare to dream and take a risk ... Those are what's instrumental," he says. "Those are what's needed to develop products that will change the world."

David works in his lab.

David tinkers with the mechanics.

a prosthetic leg developed by David

DESIGNING **PROSTHETIC SOCKETS** WAS A PROJECT DAVID STARTED IN **GRADUATE SCHOOL** AT THE MASSACHUSETTS INSTITUTE OF TECHNOLOGY (MIT).

ONE OF DAVID'S EARLY DESIGNS **BROKE** WHEN HIS PROFESSOR WAS TRYING IT OUT, BUT THE PROFESSOR DIDN'T GIVE DAVID A BAD GRADE. THEY JUST WORKED TOGETHER TO FIX IT.

DAVID **DESIGNS HIS OWN CLOTHES** AND OWNS A CLOTHING STORE IN SIERRA LEONE CALLED NYALI CLOTHING NYALI MEANS **"MY HEART"** IN MENDE, ONE OF THE LANGUAGES SPOKEN IN HIS HOME COUNTRY

CAUGHT IN THE TRACTOR!

Are TRACTOR BEAMS real? How do they work?

Check It Out!

It's one of the most awesome tools of a starship: a beam of energy that grabs something and moves it around. But that's just sci-fi, right? Not anymore. Scientists right here on Earth have built real-life tractor beams. Don't expect to use one to pull a starship any time soon—or even a toy helicopter. Tractor beams only move really small stuff for now. But they still may do all sorts of cool things, like battle viruses or clean up pollution. See what happens when a tractor beam locks on.

How do tractor beams grab and pull things **?**

How far can tractor beams go **?**

Can I beam myself a snack while I'm watching TV **?**

JUST THE FACTS

Getting a Grip

One of the coolest tractor beams shoots out laser light that's shaped like a doughnut! You trap what you want to move inside the beam's "doughnut hole." Then you can move it back and forth inside the beam. But how? Does the tractor beam use little hooks? Magnets? Magic? No, none of those. It uses heat energy. When something gets heated up, its insides get really jiggly. If it jiggles so much that it bumps into something, it bounces away in the opposite direction. Lasers can aim really, really well, so you can heat up the exact spots you want to make jiggle more. If you want to scoot a trapped object up a tractor beam, just heat up the trapped object's opposite side! It's like you're chasing it with a heat ray.

Mighty Micromover

Even if real tractor beams can only grab tiny things, they still can be powerful tools. Doctors could use them some-day to carry medicine to exactly where our bodies need it. In science labs, tractor beams could hold danger-ous particles for scientists to study. They might even be able to pull pollution out of the air. If they're mounted on rovers, they could explore hard-to-reach places, like volcanoes, the deep sea, or distant planets.

Making Waves

Doughnut-shaped tractor beams have competition. Other scientists are developing different types of laser-light tractor beams. Several designs use two laser beams. One works like laser chopsticks, and another creates target-shaped beams with multiple rings. But that's not all. One team of researchers also made sound waves pull objects. Another team created a water tractor beam that draws floating objects toward them.

SOURCE:
High-powered, concentrated laser light is created.

THINK BIG

A UFO uses a ray of light to abduct a sleeping farmer through his bedroom window. The U.S.S. *Enterprise* tows other ships through space with a beam. We see tractor beams do some pretty amazing stuff on TV, but how much power would we really need to make it happen? **We went to experts at NASA and NYU to find out!**

FUN FACT

SCIENTISTS IN THE **1960s** FIGURED OUT IN THEORY—THAT IS, THEY THOUGHT UP THE IDEAS—HOW TO MAKE TRACTOR BEAMS, BUT IT WASN'T UNTIL THE **2010s** THAT THEY COULD MAKE ONE WORK IN REAL LIFE.

INSIDE THE BEAM

You'll never look at doughnuts the same way again.
This doughnut-shaped tractor beam traps an object inside its
"doughnut hole" and moves it around using heat energy.

PLATES:
Special plates control how the laser light waves.

OBJECT:
The beam traps an object in the center, or "hole," of its doughnut shape.

BEAM:
The laser shoots out a doughnut-shaped tractor beam.

NASA may want tractor beams to help pick up trash. OK, not simple trash, but **"ORBITAL DEBRIS,"** everything from dead satellites floating in space to tiny bits of paint that have chipped off spacecraft. Maybe tractor beams will end up on spacecraft after all.

"Laser" is an acronym for "**L**ight **A**mplification by **S**timulated **E**mission of **R**adiation." Go on, impress your friends.

100 watts of laser power can pull an object less than a third of an inch (10 mm) across, like a small button, about a meter.

What's **100 watts?** Nothing too unusual. Plenty of incandescent lightbulbs use 100 watts—but they aren't giving off 100 watts of extremely efficient, focused laser light.

Lifting something as large as Just a baseball would require a gigawatt—that's **1,000,000,000 watts.** And that's ignoring the fact that a gigawatt is actually enough power to totally vaporize the baseball.

Speaking of science fiction, **one gigawatt** is just under the amount of power the DeLorean needed to travel through time in *Back to the Future.*

So what does that mean for spaceship towing and alien abductions? Well, first it means that they would take **waaaay more power**—we're talking some huge numbers. And secondly, don't expect to see tractor beams doing these feats any time soon!

FUN FACT

THE EARLIEST REFERENCE TO A TRACTOR BEAM MAY HAVE BEEN BY SCIENCE-FICTION WRITER **EDWARD E. "DOC" SMITH,** WHOSE STORY "THE SKYLARK OF SPACE," SERIALIZED IN 1928, REFERS TO AN "ATTRACTOR BEAM."

WANT TO KNOW MORE?

TELL ME MORE

HEAT IS EXCITING. LITERALLY!

If we could see the microscopic gas particles inside air, we'd see them jiggling and bumping into and bouncing off everything nearby. Heat them up, and they fly around faster and faster. When a particle jumps up a level in energy, like when it's heated, scientists say it's "excited." (Yes, that's the highly technical scientific term.) The doughnut-shaped tractor beam uses that aspect of heat energy to its advantage. It targets spots on the object it wants to move and also in the air nearby, and it heats them up. When the heated gas particles in the air crash into the object's hot spots, they shoot off with extra energy, pushing the object in the opposite direction. The particles are literally excited to do the work.

A NEW TWIST

How does a laser beam heat the far side of something without blasting a hole through it or heating its front first? To answer this question, you first need to know how laser light is special. Light travels in waves of energy. Most light waves—like from the sun or a lightbulb—vibrate every which way. A laser beam is different. Its light is polarized, meaning it vibrates in just one direction or plane. The doughnut-shaped tractor beam takes that a step further. Its laser light can vibrate in really weird ways. Imagine that the doughnut-shaped laser beam is like a tiny bike wheel. As the laser light streams forward, its light waves can vibrate different ways: either along the spokes or along the rim of the wheel. When they curve around the rim, they corkscrew around the object and reach its far side.

FUN FACTS

● The doughnut-shaped tractor beam made headlines for moving an object about **100 times** farther than previous experiments had. **Wow!** How far did it go, you ask? Well ... uh ... not quite **8 inches** (about 20 cm). And the object it moved was a hollow glass ball about the **width of two human hairs.** But, still, it moved it with only laser energy. **Awesome.**

● Researchers haven't been able to **test** how far their doughnut-shaped tractor beam can beam. **Their lab wasn't big** enough.

TRY THIS!

Stretch a Slinky out. (This is easiest with a partner, but you can do it alone if you attach it to something.) Give your hand a quick shake up and down. How does the Slinky move? Do you see a wave travel down it? If you think about it, two things are going on. Energy travels from you to the other end. At the same time, the Slinky vibrates up and down. That's how laser light acts. Now move your hand as if you're twirling a jump rope. Do you see a circular wave travel down the Slinky? That's more like the weird ways the doughnut-shaped tractor beam makes its light waves move.

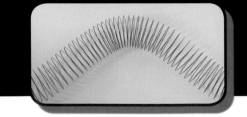

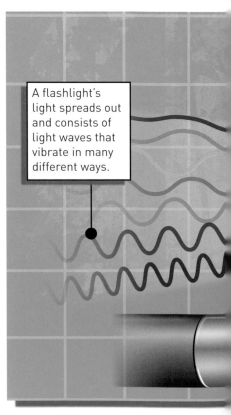

A flashlight's light spreads out and consists of light waves that vibrate in many different ways.

STRANGE VIBRATIONS

The creators of the doughnut-shaped tractor beam added some strange twists to the way laser light waves vibrate. The changes make it possible for them to target areas to heat up.

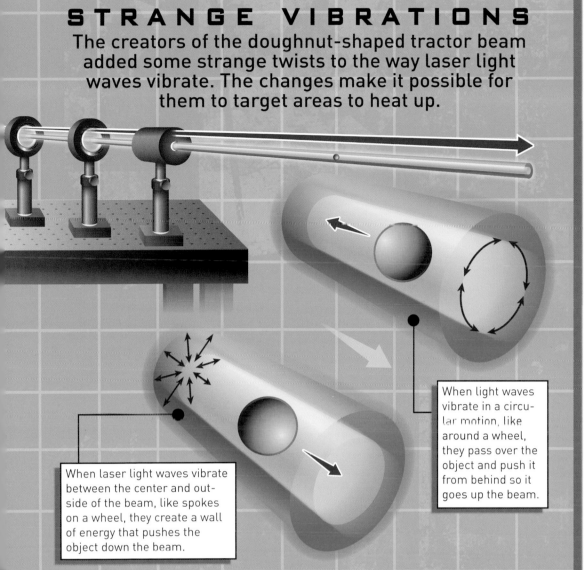

When light waves vibrate in a circular motion, like around a wheel, they pass over the object and push it from behind so it goes up the beam.

When laser light waves vibrate between the center and outside of the beam, like spokes on a wheel, they create a wall of energy that pushes the object down the beam.

ILLUMINATING DIFFERENCES

Laser light works very differently from regular light, like from the sun or a flashlight.

A laser's light is concentrated in a powerful, tight beam, and its light waves vibrate together in just one direction or plane.

TRY THIS!

VANISHING ACT:

MAKE A CLOAKING DEVICE WITH MIRRORS

It's a magician's secret: how to make something vanish. Nothing disappears "into thin air," it just disappears from sight. That's what cloaking is, and you'll do it here with mirrors. You can't carry this cloaking device around with you, but it's the easiest way to make something invisible—at least for now.

WHAT YOU NEED

TIME: about an hour

Ask an adult to help.

1. 4 rectangular unframed mirrors with smooth edges, all the same size (any size works, but bigger ones are more fun! Grab a grown-up if you're using big ones.)

2. duct tape

3. 2 objects taller than the mirrors

42

1. FIND A PLACE WHERE YOU can set up the mirrors and look at them from a distance. For big mirrors, a wide hallway works great.

2. LAY TWO MIRRORS on a flat surface, shiny side down. Leave enough space between the mirrors so they can bend easily and tape their edges together with duct tape. Repeat with the other set of mirrors.

3. LINE UP the two sets of mirrors, as in the diagram. The shiny surfaces of the two sets of mirrors must face each other, and the corners should point off to the side. **Tip:** Line up the mirrors exactly. A good way to do this is to measure how far apart they are in several places. The distance should be the same everywhere. (Try to hide the first set of mirrors off to the side, so no one can see the back of the mirror.)

4. PLACE SOMETHING (or someone) inside the cloaking region (inside the "L" of the second, shiny-side-out set of mirrors). Place something else directly behind the first object, but on the far side of the mirrors.

5. LOOK AT THE MIRRORS from the side, so the corners are pointing to your right or left. **Tip:** Pretend there's a line going from the corner of the first set of mirrors to the corner of the second set, like the top of a "T" on its side. You need to be at the bottom of the T's stem.

TIP: Try mirrors of different sizes and dimensions! See how these changes can affect the illusion.

WE MAY HAVE TO WORK HARD TO BECOME INVISIBLE, BUT MANY INSECTS HAVE BUILT-IN CLOAKING DEVICES! WALKING STICK INSECTS LOOK JUST LIKE ... WELL, STICKS. THEY EVEN MOVE LIKE SWAYING TREE BRANCHES TO AVOID BEING FOUND OUT.

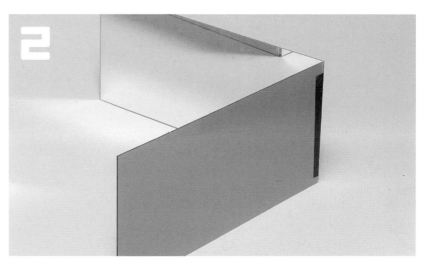

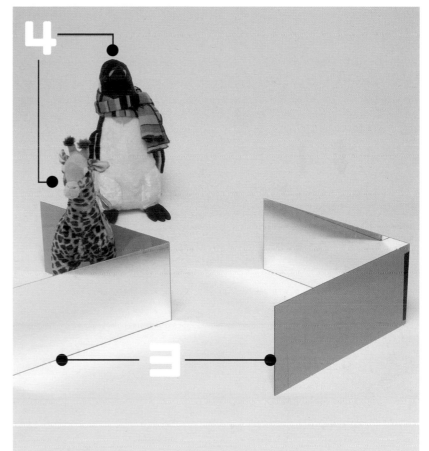

YOU CAN'T SEE WHAT YOU PUT IN THE CLOAKING REGION. YOU SEE WHATEVER'S ON THE FAR SIDE OF THE MIRRORS. DIDN'T WORK? MAKE SURE TO PLAY AROUND WITH THE ANGLES OF THE MIRRORS. ALSO TRY PLAYING AROUND WITH HOW CLOSE AND HIGH YOU ARE LOOKING AT THEM.

CLOAKING IS A TRICK OF LIGHT. WE ONLY SEE THINGS WHEN LIGHT BOUNCES OFF THEM AND HITS OUR EYES. IN THIS EXPERIMENT, YOU'RE MAKING LIGHT GO AROUND THE THING YOU'RE CLOAKING. YOU CAN SEE WHAT'S BEHIND IT, BECAUSE THE MIRRORS LET THAT LIGHT BOUNCE BACK TO YOU.

CHAPTER 2

Home is WHERE THE FRIDGE IS.

You've heard it a million times:
THERE'S NO PLACE LIKE HOME.

It's not just a house or apartment. It's more than a place we crash at night. It's where our dogs run to greet us, our cats ignore us, and our fish show off. It's stuffed with our stuff. It's toy central. It's our go-to place for family fun night. And food. Definitely food. It's where we keep it, cook it, eat it, and get rid of it after our bodies are done with it. It's home. And it's where the fridge is.

KING OF COOL

How does a REFRIGERATOR work?

Check It Out!

Looking for a midnight snack? You know where to turn: your trusty fridge. When it comes to cold food, the fridge is supercool. But have you ever wondered how it works? How does that big box manage to keep everything inside at the perfect chilly temperature even on the hottest days? Get ready to find out why your fridge is the king of cool.

How does a fridge remain at the same temperature inside?

Why is the air cold?

What are those coils for on the back of the fridge?

JUST THE FACTS

Keeping It Cool

You may think your fridge is just standing there, but part of it is constantly on the move. A special chemical refrigerant (or coolant) loops through a pipe from the inside of your fridge to the outside and back again.

A compressor, powered by electricity, pumps the refrigerant through the pipe over and over again. Along the way, the refrigerant picks up heat inside the fridge at the evaporator coils. It then carries the heat outside to the grill-like condenser coils, where it gets rid of the heat. The refrigerant returns to the fridge through an expansion valve and does it all again. Voilà! Your milk stays fresh.

Uh-Oh! The Power Is Out!

When your power goes out from a storm, do your parents tell you to keep the fridge closed? That's because electricity runs the fridge. When your electricity goes out, there's no way to get rid of any heat inside the fridge. When it's not running, your fridge acts just like a big cooler. It's insulated so it holds the chill inside for a while. But if you open the fridge door, you let heat in. And that can lead to lots of spoiled food.

HAVE YOU EVER HEARD anyone refer to a fridge as an **"ICEBOX"**? Back in the early days of refrigeration, the fridge used **A BLOCK OF ICE** to cool the air inside.

TO FRIDGE OR NOT TO FRIDGE?

YES

NO

So why do we need fridges at all? Well, for one thing, keeping food cool keeps it from spoiling. You wouldn't want that piece of meat hanging out on the counter for weeks! There are some foods, though, that fall into a do-they-don't-they zone. Peanut butter, for example, won't spoil if it's left out. Yet, some people do refrigerate it! **So, we asked 100 people: Do you refrigerate peanut butter?**

FUN FACT

DID YOU KNOW THAT **ALBERT EINSTEIN CO-INVENTED A REFRIGERATOR?** HE AND HIS FORMER STUDENT LEO SZILARD RECEIVED **A PATENT FOR IT IN 1930.**

WHAT'S INSIDE?

Let's shed some light on what's inside the fridge
(besides week-old Chinese food).

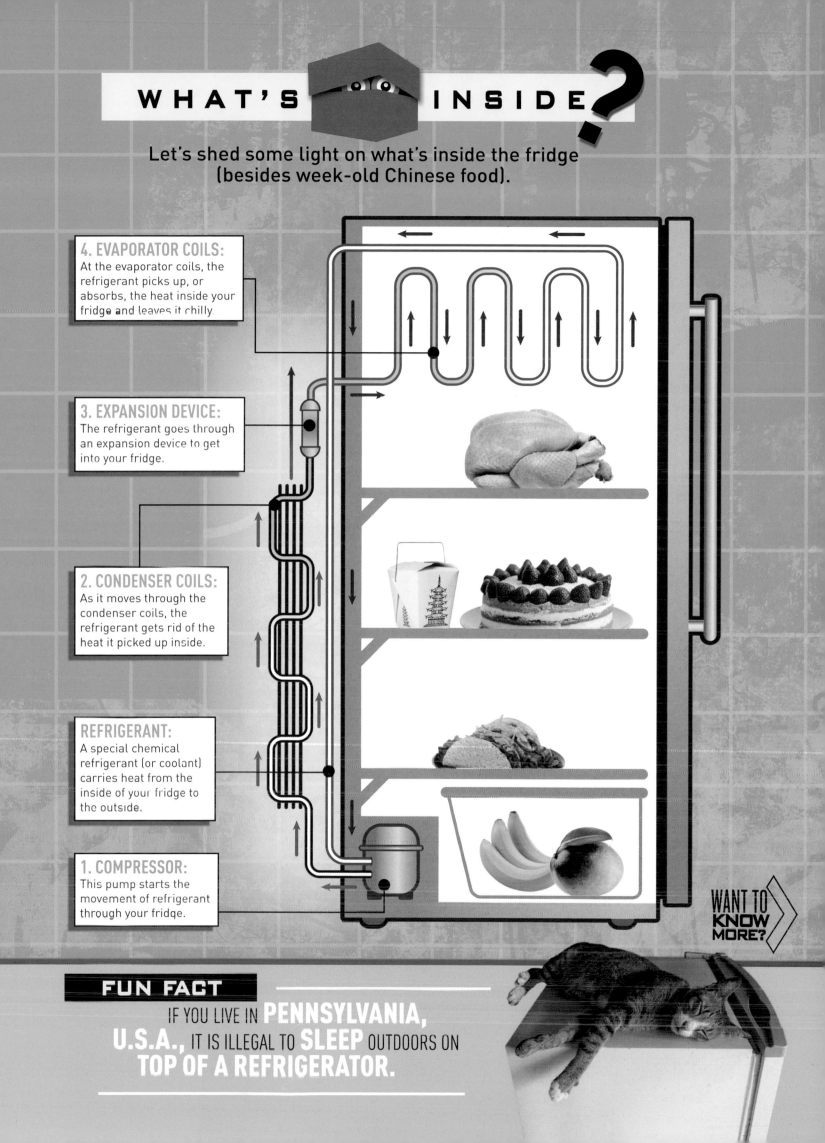

4. EVAPORATOR COILS:
At the evaporator coils, the refrigerant picks up, or absorbs, the heat inside your fridge and leaves it chilly.

3. EXPANSION DEVICE:
The refrigerant goes through an expansion device to get into your fridge.

2. CONDENSER COILS:
As it moves through the condenser coils, the refrigerant gets rid of the heat it picked up inside.

REFRIGERANT:
A special chemical refrigerant (or coolant) carries heat from the inside of your fridge to the outside.

1. COMPRESSOR:
This pump starts the movement of refrigerant through your fridge.

WANT TO KNOW MORE?

FUN FACT

IF YOU LIVE IN **PENNSYLVANIA, U.S.A.,** IT IS ILLEGAL TO **SLEEP** OUTDOORS ON **TOP OF A REFRIGERATOR.**

TELL ME MORE

MASTER OF CHANGE

The refrigerant uses a cool trick to get rid of heat. As it loops through your fridge, it changes from hot to cold and back. Why's that important? When a hot thing is next to something cold, its heat moves into the cold object and warms it up. Whatever loses the heat cools down. When the refrigerant is inside your fridge, it's cool. So it absorbs heat and leaves the fridge cooler. When the refrigerant goes outside to your fridge's condenser coils, it loses its heat to the surrounding, cooler air. How can refrigerant be cool sometimes and hot at other times? While it loops through your fridge, it turns from a liquid to a gas (evaporation) and then back again from a gas to a liquid (condensation). In the evaporator coils, the liquid refrigerant absorbs so much heat that it turns into a gas. When it loses its heat in the condenser coils, it turns back into a liquid. Then it does it all over again.

ON AGAIN, OFF AGAIN

If you've noticed your refrigerator running for a while, then turning itself off, then doing it again and again, thank a little gadget inside your fridge called a thermocouple (basically a thermometer). When it senses that your fridge is cold enough, it turns off the power to the compressor. When heat sneaks into your fridge—either when you open the door or through leaky places around the doors and pipes—the thermocouple signals the compressor to get back to work.

TRY THIS!

If you put a little rubbing alcohol on your skin, you'll feel a chill. Ever wonder why? When the rubbing alcohol evaporates, changing from a liquid to a gas that floats away, it takes along some of the heat from your skin. It leaves the chill behind. That's what the refrigerant does when it goes through the evaporator coils in your fridge. It evaporates inside the coils, taking the heat from inside the fridge along with it.

You may soon be able to stick a snack in this gooey gel fridge from Electrolux!

● In 2010, **Russian** designer Yuriy Dmitriev came up with a prototype for **a radical new way** to keep foods cold. **His Bio Robot Refrigerator uses a special green gooey gel** that holds and cools food. The fridge doesn't need doors, drawers, or **even a motor.**

● Refrigerators have their own holiday! Kind of. **November 15 is National Clean Out Your Refrigerator Day** in the United States. Don't forget to make a card.

THE COOL CYCLE
Check out how your fridge chills out.

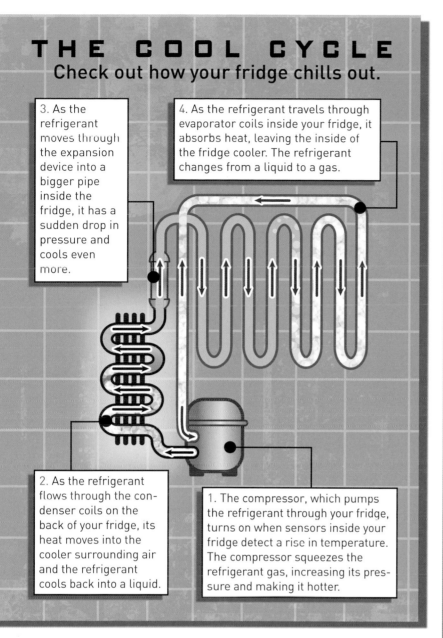

3. As the refrigerant moves through the expansion device into a bigger pipe inside the fridge, it has a sudden drop in pressure and cools even more.

4. As the refrigerant travels through evaporator coils inside your fridge, it absorbs heat, leaving the inside of the fridge cooler. The refrigerant changes from a liquid to a gas.

2. As the refrigerant flows through the condenser coils on the back of your fridge, its heat moves into the cooler surrounding air and the refrigerant cools back into a liquid.

1. The compressor, which pumps the refrigerant through your fridge, turns on when sensors inside your fridge detect a rise in temperature. The compressor squeezes the refrigerant gas, increasing its pressure and making it hotter.

● A woman in Nevada, U.S.A., collected around **45,000 refrigerator magnets**—enough to earn her a **Guinness World Record.** She must have a magnetic personality.

● About **10 million** refrigerators are sold each year in the United States.

● If your parents ever go to the grocery store and don't remember if they are out of milk, they might like a new **camera-equipped "smart refrigerator."** They can contact the fridge using their cell phone, and it'll send them a picture of **what's inside it.**

Forgot the milk?

Whoa ... SLOW DOWN!
A Closer Look at the States of Matter

During its journey through your fridge, refrigerant turns from a liquid to a gas back to a liquid again. That sounds cool, but what does it really mean?

Let's start from the beginning: If you took an ice cube and broke it up into its tiniest pieces, you'd have molecules. Molecules are made up of atoms bonded together, and in a solid state (such as our ice cube), these molecules can't move past each other. That's why a solid keeps its size and shape.

When you heat something up, the extra energy from the heat makes the molecules start to move faster. So as our ice cube sits on the counter, it gains heat from the air around it. Its molecules start to vibrate more and slide past one another—the water keeps its size but not its shape. This solid is becoming a liquid.

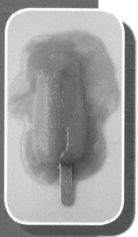

Now say we heat the liquid water up even more by boiling it in a pot. The extra energy from the stove will make the water's molecules go crazy. They'll wiggle around at high speeds and move freely past each other, causing the liquid water to become a gas. Now the water has no definite size and shape.

As matter takes in energy as it changes from solid to liquid to gas, it makes the environment around it cooler. As it releases energy as it goes from gas to liquid to solid, it makes the environment around it warmer. Together, that tag team process helps your fridge stay nice and cool.

Ice pops are mostly water.

SOMETHING'S FISHY

How does an AQUARIUM become a fish habitat?

Check It Out!

It's way more than a simple fish tank. An aquarium is a little aquatic world inside your home. It has special equipment to keep your fish healthy and happy. Some parts bubble, some clean the water, and some make your fish comfy. Have you ever wondered how they work? Dive in to find out what it takes to make your finny friends feel at home.

What are all those tubes for?

Who cleans up after the fish?

Why do some decorations make bubbles?

JUST THE FACTS

Homemakers

A lot of equipment works together to create a safe habitat for healthy fish. A heater keeps the water at a steady temperature (76 to 80 degrees Fahrenheit, or 24 to 27 degrees Celsius, for tropical fish). A filter, either under the tank or hanging on its back, helps to clean the water. Air pumps or "bubblers" help to circulate the water, which spreads oxygen more evenly through the tank. Decorations provide hiding places for your fish, so they don't get stressed. Happy fish are healthy fish—and are more likely to show off.

The **SHANGHAI OCEAN AQUARIUM** in China has an underwater tunnel that's longer than one and a half **FOOTBALL FIELDS.** It lets visitors get extra close to sharks and other fish.

What's Lurking in the Gravel?

Fish aren't the only creatures living in your aquarium. A lot of microscopic bacteria live there, too—and that's a good thing! Some bacteria help keep the tank's water safe for the fish. The bacteria gobble up fish waste and convert it into less harmful products.

NEW FISH IN TOWN

Thinking about putting together your own **freshwater aquarium?** If that's the case, you might not know where to start. You know all about how aquariums work, but what about the fish? Check out these fish that are great for a starter freshwater aquarium!

SWORDTAIL
- **LIFE SPAN:** about 3 years
- **SIZE:** up to 6 inches (15 cm) long
- **FAVORITE WATER TEMPERATURE:** 64°F–82°F (18°C–28°C)

Swordtails can have 80 babies at once!

GUPPY
- **LIFE SPAN:** 1 to 3 years
- **SIZE:** up to 1.5 inches (3.8 cm) long
- **FAVORITE WATER TEMPERATURE:** 72°F–82°F (22°C–28°C)

NEON TETRA
- **LIFE SPAN:** 2 to 5 years
- **SIZE:** 1.25 inches (3 cm) long
- **FAVORITE WATER TEMPERATURE:** 68°F–78°F (20°C–26°C)

There are lots of different colors and types of tetras, making up hundreds of distinct species.

FUN FACT

FISH ARE **GOOD FOR YOU**—AND NOT JUST THE KIND YOU CAN EAT. RESEARCH HAS SHOWN THAT WATCHING FISH IN AN AQUARIUM HELPS **LOWER STRESS.**

AQUA ECOSYSTEM

Let's dive in to the details of how an aquarium keeps your pet fish happy and healthy.

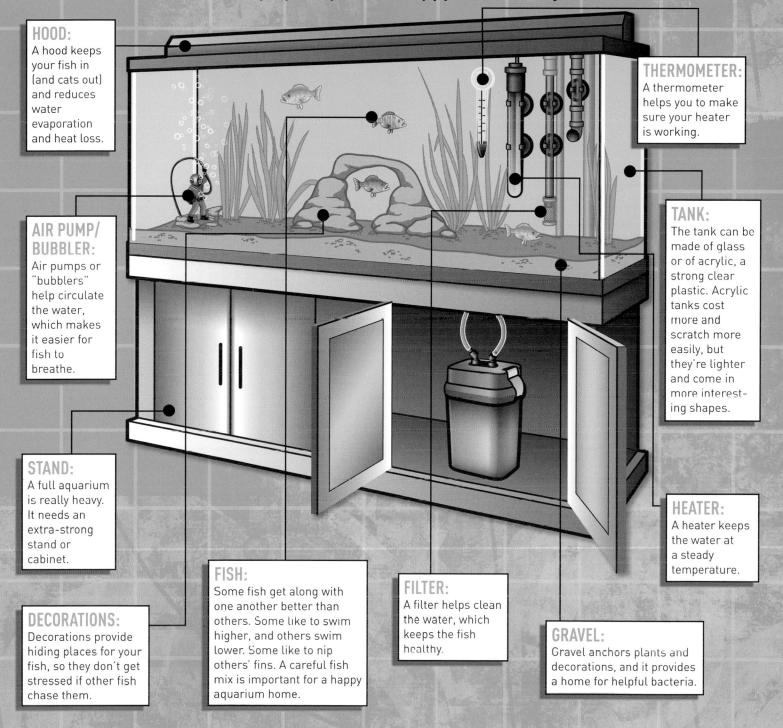

HOOD:
A hood keeps your fish in (and cats out) and reduces water evaporation and heat loss.

THERMOMETER:
A thermometer helps you to make sure your heater is working.

AIR PUMP/ BUBBLER:
Air pumps or "bubblers" help circulate the water, which makes it easier for fish to breathe.

TANK:
The tank can be made of glass or of acrylic, a strong clear plastic. Acrylic tanks cost more and scratch more easily, but they're lighter and come in more interesting shapes.

STAND:
A full aquarium is really heavy. It needs an extra-strong stand or cabinet.

HEATER:
A heater keeps the water at a steady temperature.

DECORATIONS:
Decorations provide hiding places for your fish, so they don't get stressed if other fish chase them.

FISH:
Some fish get along with one another better than others. Some like to swim higher, and others swim lower. Some like to nip others' fins. A careful fish mix is important for a happy aquarium home.

FILTER:
A filter helps clean the water, which keeps the fish healthy.

GRAVEL:
Gravel anchors plants and decorations, and it provides a home for helpful bacteria.

FUN FACT

GENERALLY, EVERY INCH (2.5 CM) OF FISH **REQUIRES A GALLON** (ALMOST 4 LITERS) OF WATER. TO FIGURE OUT HOW BIG A TANK TO GET, FIND OUT HOW LONG YOUR FISH WILL BE **WHEN THEY'RE GROWN** AND THEN ADD UP ALL THOSE MEASUREMENTS.

WANT TO **KNOW MORE?**

TELL ME MORE

FISH TOILET

Fish eat, which means—you guessed it—that stuff comes out the other end, too. If the fish live in a river or ocean, there's no problem. Water currents flush away their waste. But if they live in an aquarium, a filter helps do the job. Filters clean the water by removing fish waste, rotting leftover food, decaying plants, dangerous chemicals, and other gross things. If those things are left in the tank, they create a buildup of ammonia, a chemical compound that makes it hard for fish to breathe. Filters help make a safe home for fish, but they can't do it all alone. You still need to change the aquarium water on a regular basis.

CLEAN MACHINE
The most powerful filters clean aquarium water several ways.

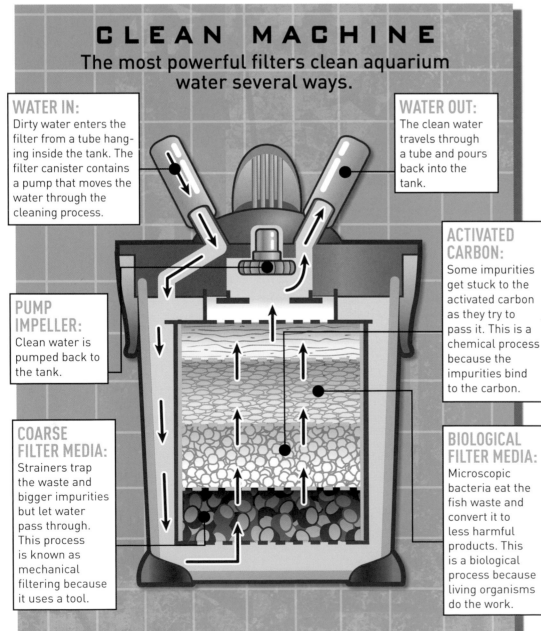

WATER IN:
Dirty water enters the filter from a tube hanging inside the tank. The filter canister contains a pump that moves the water through the cleaning process.

WATER OUT:
The clean water travels through a tube and pours back into the tank.

PUMP IMPELLER:
Clean water is pumped back to the tank.

ACTIVATED CARBON:
Some impurities get stuck to the activated carbon as they try to pass it. This is a chemical process because the impurities bind to the carbon.

COARSE FILTER MEDIA:
Strainers trap the waste and bigger impurities but let water pass through. This process is known as mechanical filtering because it uses a tool.

BIOLOGICAL FILTER MEDIA:
Microscopic bacteria eat the fish waste and convert it to less harmful products. This is a biological process because living organisms do the work.

TRY THIS!

If you have a coffee drinker in the house, you can try a cool experiment. Fill two clear glasses with water and put a straw in the second glass. Add half a teaspoon (about 3 ml) of ground coffee to each glass but don't mix it in. (If you don't have ground coffee, try ground pepper. It works pretty well, too.) Blow through the straw to make bubbles, and then compare the two glasses. The coffee sits on top of the water in the first glass, but it swirls around the water in the second glass with a straw. The coffee is acting a bit like the oxygen in a fish tank. There's more at the water's surface, where it comes into contact with air. But the bubbler in an aquarium—like your straw—moves the water around so the oxygen is spread more evenly through the water. That's a nice thing to do for fish.

NO SCUBA NECESSARY

Fish need oxygen to breathe, just like people do. So how do they get that oxygen? Fish can't use lungs like ours, because our lungs won't work if they're filled with fluid. Lucky for fish, they have the perfect organs for their habitat: gills.

Gills are feathery organs full of blood vessels. To breathe, a fish makes water flow from its mouth through its gills. When the water passes through the gills, the oxygen moves from the water into the fish's bloodstream.

How Things Worked

Ancient Egyptian art showed sacred fish kept in rectangular pools at temples, and the Chinese and Japanese raised colorful koi and goldfish 2,000 years ago just for fun. Carp pools also were a hit in medieval European estates and monasteries—both for food and pleasure. These early fish keepers relied on the ponds' natural habitats to keep the fish alive. Helpful bacteria turned fish waste into food for plants. The plants filtered the water, supplied oxygen, and provided food for the fish. Back then, people didn't understand how it all worked. They just knew it did. By the Tang Dynasty, A.D. 618–907, the Chinese brought their favorite fish inside to display in large ceramic containers—the first fish bowls. But they no doubt learned that the fish needed to go back outside to stay alive. By the mid-1700s, Europeans kept goldfish in glass bowls, but it wasn't until the early 1800s that fish owners understood how to make a healthy indoor fish habitat.

a Chinese vase from the 16th century

● A shopping mall in Dubai, United Arab Emirates, contains a gigantic **shark-filled** aquarium. Its side is **108 feet** (33 m) long, **27 feet** (8 m) tall, and **30 inches** (75 cm) thick. In 2010, the tank sprang a leak, forcing an evacuation and a brief shutdown of the shopping mall. No fish were hurt.

● The first **public** aquarium opened in 1853 at the **London Zoo** in England. It was stocked by British naturalist Philip Gosse, whose work launched an aquarium **craze.**

● In 1832, French **marine biologist** Jeanne Villepreux-Power invented the aquarium to **experiment** with aquatic organisms.

SNACK ZAPPER

How do MICROWAVES work?

Check It Out!

The microwave isn't as amazing as the discovery of fire, but it may come close (at least in the history of cooking). This wonderful kitchen appliance of the 1970s truly revolutionized cooking. Do you want to know why? See how a microwave oven can cook you a snack in a matter of minutes.

How does a microwave oven cook so fast?

Why can't I put my fork in there?

How does the plate stay cool?

JUST THE FACTS

What's So Special About a Microwave?

When you use a regular oven or stove, food starts cooking from the outside, the part of the food next to the hot pot or air. The heat has to work its way from the food's surface to the inside before that part can cook. Microwaves work very differently. They immediately reach all the way inside the food, so every bit of it cooks at the same time. They also get to work faster because, unlike regular ovens, microwave ovens don't have to heat up to a high temperature to start cooking. You get a yummy snack in a matter of minutes.

How Fast Is It?

Some foods cook superfast in a microwave oven. Others take longer. The time depends on several factors: how well the food absorbs microwaves—high-powered radio waves; how well it retains heat; and its size, shape, and original temperature. Liquids absorb microwaves easily, so they heat up faster. It's also hard for microwaves to penetrate really thick hunks of food, so it's best to cut them into bite-size bits. Spreading food on a plate also speeds its cooking.

→ 6 hours

HOT POTATO

So how much faster do microwaves cook your food, really? Turns out we haven't been exaggerating—just take a look at **how long it can take to bake a potato** with different ovens!

→ 10 minutes

MICROWAVE

→ 30 minutes

CAMPFIRE

→ 1 hour

CONVENTIONAL OVEN

SLOW COOKER

WHERE ARE THE WAVES?

Take a look inside to see how your microwave cooks some soup in a matter of minutes.

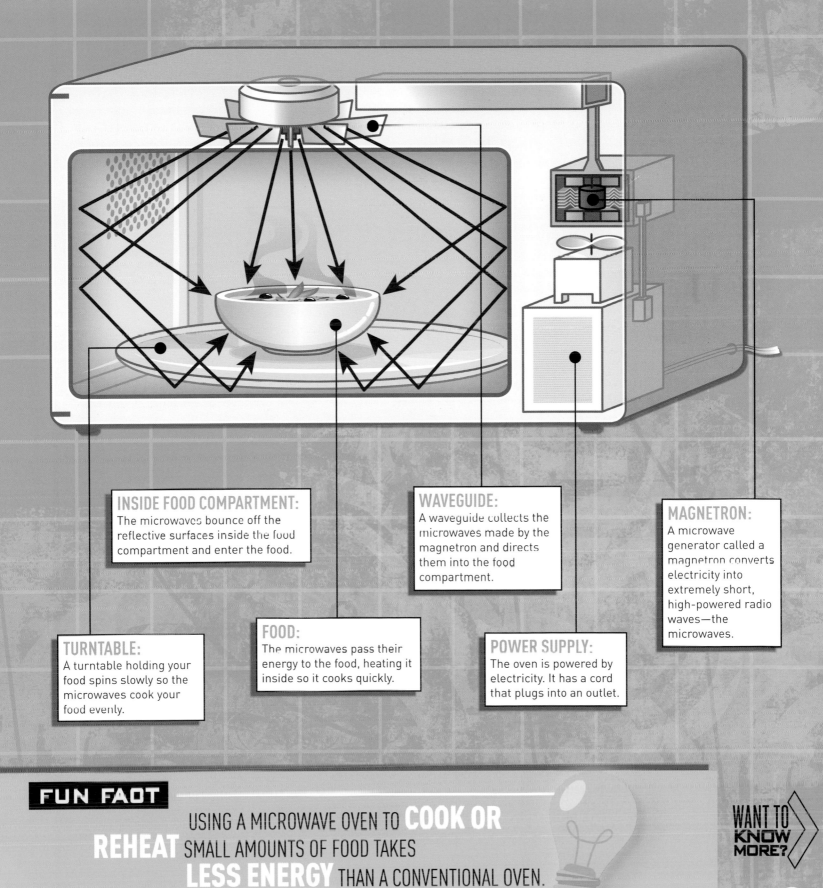

INSIDE FOOD COMPARTMENT:
The microwaves bounce off the reflective surfaces inside the food compartment and enter the food.

WAVEGUIDE:
A waveguide collects the microwaves made by the magnetron and directs them into the food compartment.

MAGNETRON:
A microwave generator called a magnetron converts electricity into extremely short, high-powered radio waves—the microwaves.

TURNTABLE:
A turntable holding your food spins slowly so the microwaves cook your food evenly.

FOOD:
The microwaves pass their energy to the food, heating it inside so it cooks quickly.

POWER SUPPLY:
The oven is powered by electricity. It has a cord that plugs into an outlet.

FUN FACT

USING A MICROWAVE OVEN TO **COOK OR REHEAT** SMALL AMOUNTS OF FOOD TAKES **LESS ENERGY** THAN A CONVENTIONAL OVEN.

WANT TO
KNOW
MORE?

TELL ME MORE...

JIGGLING FOOD

Microwaves are high-powered radio waves generated by a gadget called a magnetron. They have special properties that make them excellent at cooking food quickly. Microwaves don't stop when they hit food. They go right inside, where they pass their energy to the food's molecules, the smallest particles of the food. Here's how: Microwaves, true to their name, are waves—really fast waves. They change direction around 2.45 billion times a second! When they enter food, they rock the molecules in the food back and forth. Vibrating molecules rub against each other, creating heat. The heat cooks your food. Delicious!

TRY THIS! (BEWARE OF HOT WATER AND STEAM!)

Which do you think is faster: making ice melt or making water boil? The temperature only has to rise a few degrees to melt ice, while water has to heat up a lot more to boil. But boiling usually wins the race! Here's why: It takes a lot of energy to break the bonds holding the ice molecules together. Ice also doesn't absorb microwaves as well as water. If you want to see for yourself, place three ice cubes in a glass and weigh it on a kitchen scale. Add water to a second glass until it weighs the same as the ice glass. Position both on the turntable in a microwave, the same distance from the center. Turn on the microwave for about five minutes and watch closely. When you see bubbles in the water glass, meaning it's boiling, stop the microwave. Has all the ice melted?

FUN FACTS

- Microwaves can **pass through** glass, ceramic, and paper. But **metal reflects microwaves,** so don't put your fork in a microwave oven. It can **spark** and **hurt** the oven.

- Microwaves **bounce around** the inside of the oven. If they **bump into each other,** they may not heat some parts of your food all the way. Solution: **a turntable** that rotates the food.

- In the early days of microwaves, **advertisements** showed happy families putting their microwaves **on carts** and wheeling them outside to cook—just like **barbecue grills!**

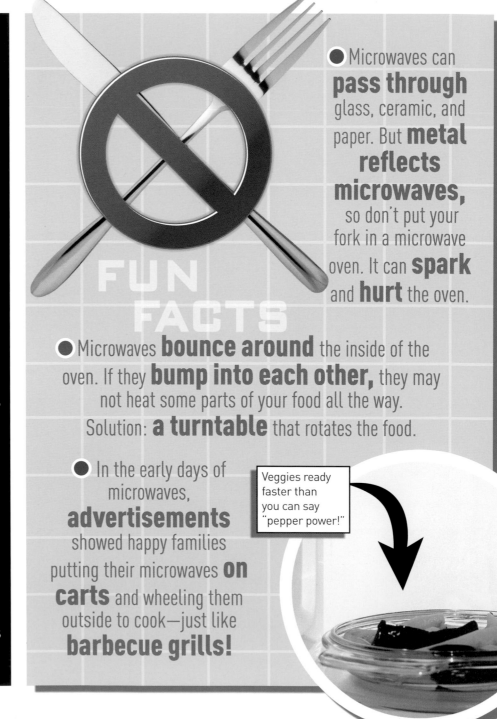

Veggies ready faster than you can say "pepper power!"

GETTING ALL JIGGLY

When microwaves enter food, they make the molecules in the food vibrate, which creates heat. The heat cooks your food.

WAVE GENERATOR

A magnetron may sound like something from science fiction, but it's actually a gadget we use every day in our homes. It's the heart of a microwave oven. Let's peek inside the tube to see how it uses electricity and magnets to make microwaves.

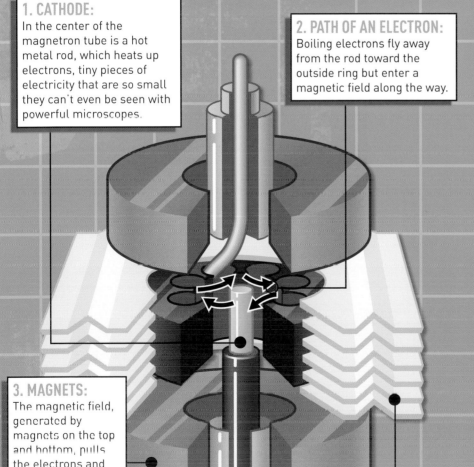

1. CATHODE:
In the center of the magnetron tube is a hot metal rod, which heats up electrons, tiny pieces of electricity that are so small they can't even be seen with powerful microscopes.

2. PATH OF AN ELECTRON:
Boiling electrons fly away from the rod toward the outside ring but enter a magnetic field along the way.

3. MAGNETS:
The magnetic field, generated by magnets on the top and bottom, pulls the electrons and swings them back toward the center, creating the microwaves.

4. COOLING FINS:
Metal "fins" keep the magnetron cool.

MYTH vs. FACT

MYTH: Zapping food with high-powered radio waves makes it less nutritious.

FACT: Relax, snack zappers, it's a myth. Here's the skinny on food nutrition: Some nutrients do break down—or lose some of their healthy characteristics—when they're heated. But guess what: It doesn't matter how they are heated. It could be in a microwave, in a regular oven, on the stove, or over a campfire. What matters more is how long you heat it. In fact, scientists have figured out that the best way to keep healthy nutrients in our food is to cook it fast, heat it up for the shortest amount of time, and use as little liquid as possible when you cook it. Let's see, what cooks fast and uses little liquid? ... The microwave! Zapping broccoli for a few minutes in a microwave is much better than boiling it in water on the stove, where its nutrients really do leach out into the cooking water. If you use your microwave right, it's one of the best ways to make sure your food keeps the vitamins and minerals that help you grow healthy and strong.

TALES FROM THE LAB

A FASTER FRANKFURTER:
THE INVENTION OF THE MICROWAVE

It started with a squirrel snack and a curious engineer. It was project "Speedie Weenie."

The engineer was Percy Spencer. Ever since he was a kid, he loved spending time outdoors. Even as an adult, he carried a peanut cluster bar in his pocket so he could feed squirrels and chipmunks during breaks at work.

He also loved machines, and he was a master at making them work better.

During World War II, Percy invented a better, faster way to make magnetrons, the electronic tubes that make microwaves. They were used in radar to help find enemy ships and airplanes, and the military needed a lot of them fast. Percy's invention was so important, the U.S. Navy gave him a medal.

PAUSING AT A PUZZLE

One day in 1945, after the war, Percy was watching a colleague test a magnetron at Raytheon, where he worked. Percy felt something weird in his pocket. It was his peanut cluster bar, and it was gooey. He wasn't near anything hot, so what melted the candy bar? The magnetron?

Most scientists in the lab would have mopped up the mess and moved on. They knew magnetrons heated things. They warmed their hands in front of magnetrons when the lab grew chilly. But no one had stopped to figure out what was going on.

Percy never passed up a puzzle. He started experimenting.

Percy put popcorn kernels near the magnetron, and big white bursts flew around the lab. He put an egg in a pot, cut a hole in the pot's side, and put it next to a magnetron. Bam! The egg exploded. It had cooked and burst out of its shell. Percy knew he had an invention.

He and his colleague Roly Hanson got to work on the "Speedie Weenie" project. They built a metal box and put magnetrons inside. The microwave oven was born.

It didn't look like what you use to zap a hot dog today. The first microwave oven, sold in 1947 to a restaurant, cost $3,000—about what most families earned in a year—and was the size of a refrigerator. It took two decades before Raytheon made a microwave oven small and cheap enough for homes. In 1967, the "Radarange" microwave cost $495—less than a month's income for most families. Within eight years, microwave ovens outsold gas stoves.

A model shows off an early microwave.

PERCY SPENCER HAD TO QUIT SCHOOL IN FIFTH GRADE AND GO TO WORK TO **HELP SUPPORT** HIS FAMILY. CURIOUS AND EAGER TO LEARN, HE TAUGHT HIMSELF **MATHEMATICS, ENGINEERING, AND SCIENCE.** HE KNEW SO MUCH THAT THE UNIVERSITY OF MASSACHUSETTS AWARDED HIM AN **HONORARY DOCTORATE** DEGREE.

BY THE 1990S, ABOUT **90 PERCENT** OF AMERICAN HOMES HAD MICROWAVE OVENS.

Percy Spencer

PERCY SPENCER PATENTED **150 INVENTIONS** AND INNOVATIONS. RAYTHEON CALLED HIM AN "INVENTIVE GENIUS, **HIGHLY RESPECTED** FOR HIS VERSATILITY" AND NAMED A BUILDING FOR HIM. HE WAS ALSO INDUCTED INTO THE **NATIONAL INVENTORS HALL OF FAME.**

Make It BETTER!

The microwave is really good at what it does. It already cooks food much faster than other ovens and doesn't need much space to do it. But don't think that all microwaves are the same—some have unique designs or special features (like knowing exactly how long popcorn should pop!) that set them apart. Others are superpowerful, and some save even more space.

Imagine the microwave you use the most. What would you change about it or add to it? Think about not only the way it looks but also its special features, technology, and function. Grab a pen and some paper, and jot down your ideas!

THE NAME "RADARANGE" WAS CHOSEN BY A RAYTHEON EMPLOYEE, WHO **WON A CONTEST** TO NAME THE NEW MICROWAVE OVEN.

Bake your pizza while you microwave popcorn? Movie Night success.

NEATNIK

How does a ROBOT VACUUM clean up after us?

Check It Out!

A little robot that zips around our homes, cleaning up after us? It's almost a dream come true. Sure, it's not Rosie from *The Jetsons*, but it's still plenty awesome. This little robot vacuum works tirelessly until it covers every last bit of our floors—and it does it without complaining. Find out why a robot vacuum is the neat helper we've always wanted.

How does it find the dirt **?**

How does it know where to go **?**

Is it really a robot **?**

67

JUST THE FACTS

On the Job

Unlike their less sophisticated relatives, robot vacuums aren't pushed around. They have to find their own way through our homes. Luckily, they have the smarts to do so. Numerous sensors help them leave their charging docks and navigate around rooms without falling down stairs or banging into furniture. It's fun watching a robot vacuum zip around the house—especially if a pet is riding it—but these little robots don't exist to entertain us. They have a job to do: cleaning up after us. Like other vacuum cleaners, they suck up dirt and dust from our carpets and floors and trap it in a bin. If only they could wash our clothes, too ...

Is It Really a Robot?

Can a vacuum cleaner really be called a robot? The Tech Museum of Innovation, in California, U.S.A., has a simple way of looking at it. A robot senses, or "thinks," and acts. It's a machine that gathers information about its environment and uses that information to follow instructions to do work. Although a robot vacuum is preprogrammed to clean, it must use the information it gathers through its sensors to figure out the best way to do its job. What do you think? Does it qualify as a robot?

Some pets love to **RIDE ROBOT VACUUMS**—but not as much as we love watching them. Videos of cats **ZIPPING AROUND** on the cleaning machines get a big audience on the Web. One was watched more than **ELEVEN MILLION TIMES.**

DOWN AND DUSTY

Your vacuum is sucking up more than just dirt and pet hair—it's actually capturing living creatures called dust mites, too! **Dust mites** live in your kitchen, in your carpet, and even on your bed, eating up the dead skin you leave behind. (Yum!) They're pretty much everywhere you go indoors, so it can't hurt to learn a thing or two about them. Check out these cool dust mite facts!

Dust mites are less than **0.5 mm** long.

3x more in BEDS
Beds are 3x more popular with dust mites than carpets are.

Pets, TOO!
It's not only humans who can be sensitive to dust mites! Of cats and dogs with allergies, up to 80% are allergic to dust mites.

TRY THIS!

If you want to see vacuum suction in action, you can do an easy experiment with a baster, the kitchen tool that's a long tube with a rubber bulb at the end. Sprinkle a little cocoa powder in a dish, and hold a tissue (only one layer!) over the pointy end of the baster. Point the baster at the cocoa and gently squeeze the bulb to get its air out (without sending the cocoa flying all over). Then hold the baster really, really close to some cocoa without touching it. Let go of the bulb quickly so it pops back into shape. Now check the tissue. Do you see a little brown spot where the baster vacuumed up the cocoa? It's fun, but not the best way to make a mug of cocoa.

INNER WORKINGS

A robot vacuum independently scoots around the house to vacuum up dirt and dust. Check out how this multitasker manages to get it all done.

DIRT BIN:
A dirt bin stores the vacuumed dirt and dust until a person empties it.

BATTERY CHARGE POINTS:
A rechargeable battery pack powers the robot vacuum. The robot automatically heads back to its charging dock after it finishes cleaning.

ROTATING BRUSHES/ EXTRACTORS:
Two brushes— or brushless dirt extractors— rotate in opposite directions to pick up dirt so the vacuum can suck it up.

WHEELS:
Two large wheels, each driven by a motor, move the vacuum. The wheels can turn in opposite directions, so the vacuum can spin around in tight places.

SIDE BRUSH:
Large side brushes sweep dirt from corners and along walls and drag it underneath the robot.

SENSORS:
Sensors detect dirt and help the robot avoid whacking furniture, falling down stairs, or getting trapped in cords or rug fringe.

WANT TO KNOW MORE?

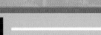

FUN FACT — WHEN THE MAKERS OF THE **ROOMBA ROBOT VACUUM** WERE TRYING TO COME UP WITH NAMES FOR THEIR INVENTION, SOME TEAM MEMBERS PROPOSED **"DUSTPUPPY"** AND **"CYBERSUCK."**

PROFILE: Helen Greiner

ENGINEER, COMPUTER SCIENTIST, ROBOTICIST

A long time ago, in a galaxy far, far away, Helen Greiner met her destiny.

She was 11 and watching the biggest hit movie of 1977: *Star Wars*. She couldn't take her eyes off one of the major characters. No, not Princess Leia or Luke Skywalker, but R2-D2, the spunky and brave little droid who whistled and bleeped his way across the galaxy.

"I was enthralled because R2-D2 was one of the main characters," she says. "He had emotions. He had a personality, and he was able to communicate without even

> ## "I DISCOVERED PRETTY QUICKLY THAT NO ONE KNEW HOW TO BUILD MOBILE ROBOTS LIKE R2-D2."

needing to speak. R2-D2 was more than a machine."

As it turned out, he wasn't a machine at all.

"I was quizzing my brother on *Star Wars* trivia—he had learned it all—and when we got to the fact that [actor] Kenny Baker played R2-D2, I said, 'What do you mean, someone played R2-D2? I thought it was a robot!'"

Helen was crushed. But she made her mind up to make a real robot someday.

She started learning the skills she'd need. Her family bought a computer, and she spent hours experimenting with it. Soon she was using it to control her brother's radio-controlled toys.

"I could see the connection between what was shown in science fiction, in *Star Wars*, and what could be built in the future with technologies that were just emerging for the computer industry."

When it was time for college, Helen went to the Massachusetts Institute of Technology (MIT), one of the best universities for science and math. She thought at last she'd learn how to make a robot.

"I discovered pretty quickly that no one knew how to build mobile robots like R2-D2," she says.

WORTH THE WAIT

Helen decided to fix that problem. Lucky for her, she met a friend and professor at MIT who also loved robots. They started a business, iRobot, and made all kinds of robots, including the Roomba robot vacuum and the PackBot, a robot that can go places that are dangerous for people.

But Helen set her goals even higher. Seriously higher.

"In the air, there is so much more free space," she says. "There are no tables or chairs to run into. Once you get above the tree level, there is really nothing else there.

It's an ideal space for robots to operate."

After 18 years at iRobot, Helen started a new business, CyPhy Works, to make flying robots. ("CyPhy" is pronounced like "Sci-Fi.")

Helen thinks flying robots will do a lot someday: see things that are difficult to reach, bring you cool drinks while you hike, or retrieve the homework you forgot to bring back to school.

Maybe they could even be your best friend. "A flying robot would be able to, like a dog, play catch with you, guard your property when you're away, and be very, very happy to see you when you get home."

Helen shows off her photo drone.

Helen stands with her PackBot.

THE GREAT PYRAMID AT GIZA WAS EXPLORED IN 2002 BY **A ROBOT DEVELOPED BY iROBOT** AND **THE NATIONAL GEOGRAPHIC SOCIETY.**

EWW, GROSS!

How does a YOU-KNOW-WHAT do its dirty work?

Check It Out!

It may be the unsung hero of our homes. It handles the stuff we don't want to, swishing it away so we don't have to give it a second thought. And it does its dirty work without complaining, day in and day out. We don't think about it unless we have to go. (You know, go.) The loo, the john, the comfort station, the facilities, the head, the lavatory, the privy, the necessary, the water closet, the porcelain throne. Call it what you will, but it's a brilliant contraption that performs one of the most valuable functions in our home. It's ... drumroll ... the toilet. There, we said it.

What does it do with the ... you know ?

How does it know when to stop ?

Why doesn't it stink a lot ?

JUST THE FACTS

Taking Care of Business

If you don't think too much about them—which is generally how we like it—toilets seem pretty straightforward. You do your business, push a handle, and—whoosh!—water pours out of the tank. When there's enough water (and other stuff) in the bowl, it all goes down the drain. Out of sight, out of mind. The drain connects to a big pipe that, thank goodness, takes the waste out of our house. Then the tank fills back up with water, so it's ready the next time "nature calls." Believe it or not, it's actually as simple as it seems.

In medieval **CASTLES,** toilets were simple benches with holes in them. These **"GARDEROBES"** were built into the **OUTSIDE WALLS** of a castle. Waste would fall from the top floors of the castle down a chute and into the moat.

That's a Lot of Flushes

The average American family of four uses 400 gallons (1,514 L) of water per day, and our toilets are the biggest water hogs. More than a fourth of the water we use every day goes down our toilets' drains. Most standard toilets use 1.6 gallons (6 L) every flush. Older toilets may use as much as 3.5 to 7 gallons (13 to 26 L) per flush! In the 1990s, the U.S. government decided we were consuming too much of a very limited resource, and so it required new toilets to use only 1.6 gallons (6 L). The U.S. Environmental Protection Agency thinks we can do even better. It estimates that if we replaced every old toilet with one that uses only 1.28 gallons (4.8 L) per flush, America would save more than 640 billion gallons (2.4 trillion L) of water per year. That's about the amount that flows over Niagara Falls in 15 days!

LOO LA LA

Most of us go to the toilet to **do our business and leave,** but not the owners of these toilets. Some toilets can even **play music,** warm your bum, and **clean up** after you. That must be why these fancy fixtures can cost thousands of dollars. They don't call it **the throne** for nothing!

DAGOBERT
The "Dagobert" Wooden Toilet Throne, named for a medieval king, stands 5 feet (1.5 m) tall, looks like a wooden throne, and costs more than $14,000. (It also includes a rustic candleholder and plays a French folk song, "Good King Dagobert," after the lid is lifted.)

CRYSTAL COMFORT
Forget about diamond rings! Toilets in the ISIS collection by designer Jemal Wright are encrusted with between 98,000 and 155,000 Swarovski crystals.

CHROME THRONE
The colorful ChromeOzone™ collection features porcelain toilets plated in bright chrome. The simplest of these seats will cost you over $5,000.

FUN FACT

THE FOLKS AT **ROTO-ROOTER** PLUMBERS, WHO PROBABLY SPEND A LOT MORE TIME **STUDYING TOILETS** THAN THE REST OF US DO, LIST **101 NAMES** FOR A TOILET ON THEIR WEBSITE.

NEAT 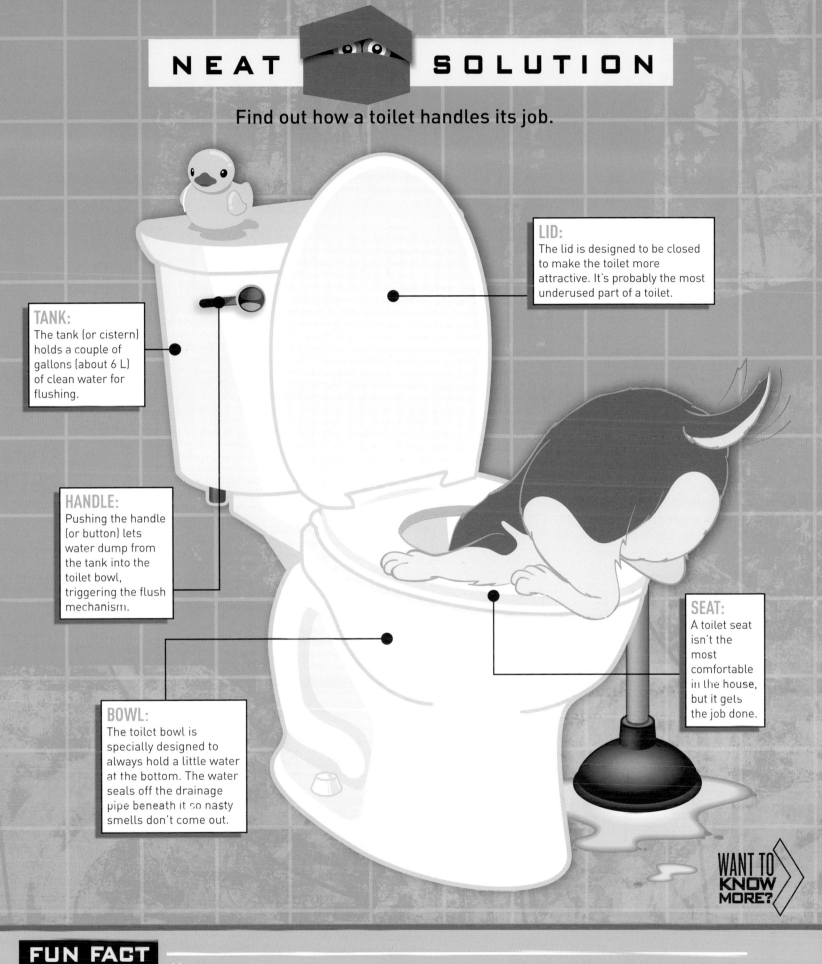 SOLUTION

Find out how a toilet handles its job.

LID:
The lid is designed to be closed to make the toilet more attractive. It's probably the most underused part of a toilet.

TANK:
The tank (or cistern) holds a couple of gallons (about 6 L) of clean water for flushing.

HANDLE:
Pushing the handle (or button) lets water dump from the tank into the toilet bowl, triggering the flush mechanism.

SEAT:
A toilet seat isn't the most comfortable in the house, but it gets the job done.

BOWL:
The toilet bowl is specially designed to always hold a little water at the bottom. The water seals off the drainage pipe beneath it so nasty smells don't come out.

WANT TO KNOW MORE?

FUN FACT

"SMART TOILETS" WITH HEATED SEATS, LIDS THAT AUTOMATICALLY OPEN WHEN YOU GET NEAR, AND **BUILT-IN DEODORIZERS** ARE PARTICULARLY POPULAR IN **JAPAN.** SOME MODELS EVEN HAVE MEDICAL SENSORS.

TELL ME MORE

BEHIND THE SCENES (GET IT? "BEHIND")

Simple is a great description of how toilets work. Toilets use a simple machine, the lever, to flush and refill the toilet. When you push the handle, a lever inside the tank pulls up a chain. The chain opens a valve called a flapper, and that lets the water pour out of the tank and into the toilet bowl. Then another lever stops the water after it refills the tank. It's connected to a float ball that rises as the water fills the tank. When the float reaches a certain level, it shuts off the refill valve for the water. Toilets also make good use of gravity, the force that pulls things toward the center of the Earth (and keeps us from floating into space). When there's enough water (and other stuff) in the toilet bowl, gravity causes everything to flow out the drain pipe. Using levers, chains, and gravity means that toilets are mechanical. They use parts moved by physical forces.

TRY THIS!

The siphon hiding inside the bottom of your toilet may be its most important part. It puts the flush into the toilet. You can see how a siphon works—without getting anywhere near the toilet. Get a foot or so (about 30 cm) of clean plastic tubing, a tall glass filled with water, and a short, empty glass. Put one end of the tube into the water and point the other end toward the empty glass. Lean down and jump-start your siphon by giving it a good suck. Watch it flow! A siphon is an upside-down U-shaped tube with one end lower than the other. It moves liquid up the tube at the high end, over the bend, and down to the lower end without using any pumps. Scientists have worked for centuries to figure out exactly how a siphon works. What's clear is that gravity provides a lot of the force that moves the liquid from one container to another. Gravity's potential energy isn't the same at the beginning and end of the tube. The difference helps keep the liquid flowing.

FUN FACTS

● A toilet made of **24-karat solid gold** is the star of an exhibit at the Hang Fung Gold Technology Company in Hong Kong. It's worth about **$5 million.** That's one posh potty!

● The **International Space Station's** toilet, built by Russia, uses leg braces to help keep astronauts properly positioned and a fan-driven **suction system** to move the waste along its way. The suction system uses **air instead of water** to flush.

The ISS

GETTING DOWN AND DIRTY

A lot is going on behind the scenes when a toilet flushes.
Find out why a toilet is the unsung hero of your home.

LEVER:
When you push on the handle, a lever inside the tank pulls up a chain.

OVERFLOW TUBE:
If something goes wrong and the refill valve does not shut off when it should, the overflow tube sends the excess water into the toilet bowl and prevents a flood in the bathroom.

FLAPPER:
The chain opens the flapper, which lets clean water rush out of the tank into the bowl. After the tank empties, the flapper settles back over the hole so the tank can refill.

FLOAT:
A float rests on top of the water in the tank. When the water flows out of the tank, the float drops and turns on the refill valve, so clean water flows back into the tank. As the tank refills, the float rises. When it reaches the right level, it shuts off the refill valve.

BOWL SIPHON:
The rush of water into the toilet bowl activates a siphon, which sucks everything in the bowl down the drain (and makes the flushing sound). As soon as the bowl empties, air enters the siphon tube and stops the siphoning process (and makes a gurgling sound).

MYTH vs. FACT

MYTH: Alligators can swim through toilet pipes and bite us *you know where.*

FACT: It's a story that makes you long for the old days, when we had to "go" in a hole in the ground. For decades, people have told of alligators that live in the sewers of New York City. As the story goes, the alligators thrive in the sewers, eating what they find down there. But, wait, you know that alligators don't live that far north. They live in wetlands, marshes, and ponds in the southern United States, right? True—except for the baby alligators that New Yorkers brought home from Florida vacations in the first half of the 1900s. Adorable souvenirs ... until they started to grow. Then the New Yorkers flushed the alligators down their toilets. In the 1930s, New York Superintendent of Sewers Teddy May said he saw them with his own eyes. So it has to be true, right? Wrong! It's a great story, but only a story. On rare occasion, an alligator—probably a former pet—turns up in and around New York City, but there's no colony in the sewers. New York's sewers get too cold in the winter, and sewage contains stuff that would make alligators sick. As for Teddy May, he was known for spinning a colorful tale. A co-worker said Teddy was "almost as much of a legend as the alligators."

TRY THIS!

WATER WONDERS:

FIND OUT WHICH FILTER WORKS BEST

How do you clean up dirty water? Not with soap! You need a filter, a device that removes impurities, like dirt, from water. The filter you'll make here is a super strainer, and it'll help you clean up your act.

WHAT YOU NEED

TIME: about an hour

Ask an adult to help.

1. 2-liter plastic bottle, empty and clean

2. Utility knife

3. Dirty water (make your own with stuff like coffee grounds, dirt, crunched-up old leaves, cooking oil, or tiny pieces of foam)

4. Measuring cup

5. Spoon

6. Stopwatch or clock with a second hand

7. Pencil and paper

8. As many of the following filter materials as you can get:
- Activated charcoal (available in the fish section at a pet store)
- Gravel
- Sand (coarse and/or fine)
- Cotton balls

9. Coffee filter (a bandanna, old sock, napkin, or paper towel works, too!)

WHAT TO DO

1. ASK A GROWN-UP to cut the bottle in half.

2. FLIP THE BOTTLE'S TOP over and put it in the bottom, so the top looks like a funnel. You'll build your filter in the top part.

3. PLACE the coffee filter (or bandanna, sock, etc.) at the bottom of your filter.

4. ADD cotton balls, charcoal, gravel, sand, and/or other materials in layers. You can use just one of them or all of them. Tip: Think about which order to add them. Bigger filter materials usually catch bigger impurities.

5. WRITE DOWN which filter materials you used and what order you layered them in.

6. STIR YOUR dirty water and measure out a cup of it.

7. GET YOUR TIMER ready.

8. POUR A CUP of dirty water into your filter. Start the timer right when you start pouring.

9. TIME HOW LONG it takes for all the water to go through the filter.

10. WRITE DOWN how long it took.

11. CAREFULLY SCOOP out the filter materials, one layer at a time. What did each layer take out of the water?

12. EXPERIMENT! Clean the bottle and try again. Put the filter materials in a different order each time. Time each experiment.

TIP: This is a fun experiment to try with other people. You can each build a filter with different materials. See whose filter takes longest and which one cleans the best.

NOTE!

YOUR FILTERED WATER IS STILL NOT CLEAN ENOUGH TO DRINK, BUT A PLANT WOULD LOVE IT.

WHAT'S GOING ON?

THE SLOWER, THE BETTER! THE LONGER IT TAKES FOR WATER TO MOVE THROUGH A FILTER, THE CLEANER IT GETS. WATER SLIPS EASILY THROUGH THE FILTER MATERIALS, BUT BIGGER GUNK, LIKE DIRT, GETS TRAPPED. THE FILTER MATERIALS USUALLY GET FINER AND FINER, SO THEY CAN CATCH WHATEVER WAS MISSED EARLIER. ACTIVATED CHARCOAL CAN BE NEAR THE END OF THE WATER'S PATH, BECAUSE IT USES AN ELECTRICAL CHARGE TO GRAB PARTICLES TOO SMALL FOR US TO SEE.

CHAPTER 3

SCHOOL OF COOL

It takes a lot of tech to
MAKE YOU A KNOW-IT-ALL.

From your humble, eraser-tipped No. 2 pencil to that futuristic interactive display at the front of your classroom, your school has the goods to help you create, learn, and explore. Technology helps make life easier and solves problems. (Too bad it won't do your homework for you!) Your teachers use it to make you even more awesome. How cool is that?

SMARTEST KID IN THE CLASS

How does your classroom's INTERACTIVE DISPLAY know so much?

Check It Out!

The interactive display is a real show-off. It knows what your teacher wants you to learn, and it plays with that information like it's a game. Whenever someone comes up with an answer, it displays it for the entire class to see. It's helping to change the way teachers teach and students learn. Now that's pretty smart.

Where does it get the information?

How can the teacher move pictures around on it?

Can I play games on it?

JUST THE FACTS

Group Project

An interactive display can't do everything by itself. It needs help from your teacher's computer and, of course, it needs someone to interact with it. The computer runs a program with the lessons your teacher wants you to learn. The display, mounted to a wall or on a special stand, shows the lesson on its big screen where you can see and interact with it. If it's an interactive whiteboard, a projector shines the computer's information on the board. Systems with newer flat-panel displays connect directly to a computer and don't need separate projectors.

What Can You Do With It?

Pretty much anything you can do on a computer, you can do on an interactive display. It's like a big touch screen on a computer or tablet. You can write or draw on it, "drag and drop" pictures and text onto the screen, change them and move them around, or watch videos. (Yes, you can play games on it, but good luck getting your teacher to let you.) Depending on the device, you control it with a special pen or just your fingers. Don't worry about your work getting lost. Teachers can save it onto their computers and even print out copies.

But Do You Learn More?

Researchers are studying whether kids learn more when they have interactive displays in their classrooms. Some studies say kids do learn more because they like getting involved with the lessons. But how much they learn depends. A good teacher is a good teacher—with or without fancy technology. The efforts that kids make matter a lot, too!

Schools in the **UNITED KINGDOM** were the first to adopt interactive displays—beating their U.S. counterparts. All U.K. classrooms have at least an interactive whiteboard, and some have multiple interactive displays.

Approximately **60 PERCENT** of U.S. classrooms had interactive display devices by 2014.

BACK TO THE DRAWING BOARD

An old saying goes that the road to the interactive display was **paved with chalk dust.** OK, maybe that's not a real saying, but it's still true. Good teachers have always found ways to get students involved in learning, whether they've had interactive displays or simple pieces of chalk. Here's a glimpse across time at innovations in classroom boards.

PRE-1800s
Students write on individual slates.

1800
James Pillans of Old High School of Edinburgh connects many slates together to teach larger geography lessons.

James Pillans

TEACHER'S AIDE

Find out how an interactive whiteboard works with a computer and projector to help you learn your lessons.

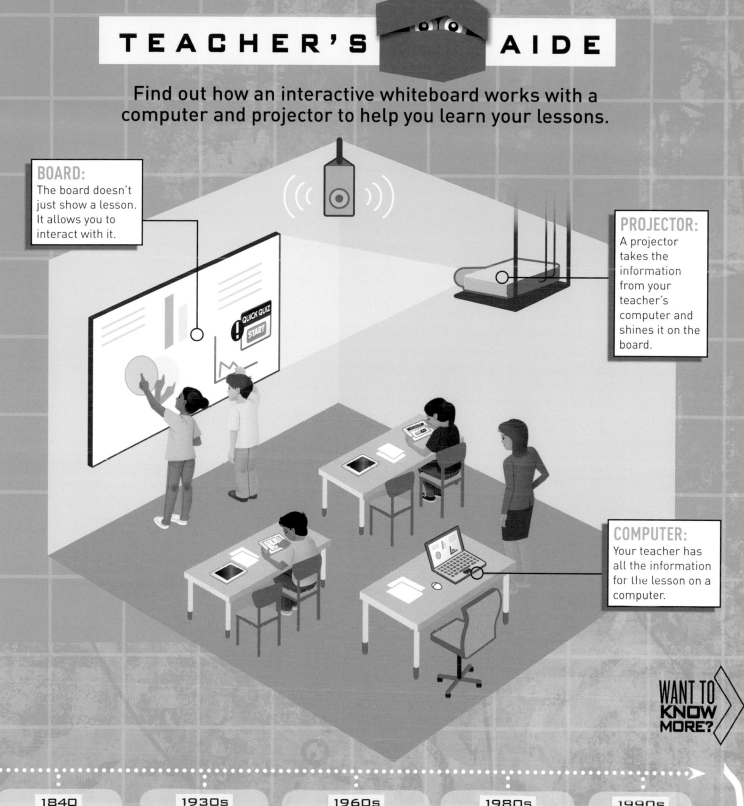

BOARD:
The board doesn't just show a lesson. It allows you to interact with it.

PROJECTOR:
A projector takes the information from your teacher's computer and shines it on the board.

COMPUTER:
Your teacher has all the information for the lesson on a computer.

QUICK QUIZ START

WANT TO KNOW MORE?

1840
Manufacturers produce blackboards that are continuous boards rather than connected slates.

1930s
Green "blackboards" are introduced to minimize glare, spurring the use of the word "chalkboard."

1960s
While earlier versions were used for training soldiers during World War II, new overhead projectors become popular in classrooms.

1980s
Whiteboards with dry-erase markers start to become common in schools because they eliminate chalk dust.

1990s
Interactive whiteboards begin to appear in offices and classrooms.

TELL ME MORE

How do interactive displays read your instructions? The first interactive whiteboards sensed where you pushed on the screen, but more recent models actually watch what you're doing. Some have little cameras in the corners of the whiteboard and computer programs to calculate the position of your fingers or pen. Other whiteboards have pens with special magnets or transmitters that send out signals to sensors in the boards.

TOUCH TV

An interactive flat panel uses the same display technology as a flat-screen television. The big difference, of course, is the panel reacts to your touch like a tablet does. You can drag your finger on the screen to write, pinch to change something's size, and swipe to move it off.

GOING TOUCHLESS

Prefer to just wave at a screen? Gesture control is becoming more common. Cameras and sensors in the screen detect and respond to different movements you make. Engineers are working on technology that even responds to your facial expressions or reads your lips. Be careful what you whisper to your best friend!

TRY THIS!

People's body language can tell us a lot about what they're thinking or feeling—or not. Picture a guy with crossed arms. It could mean he's trying to look tough, but it might mean he's shy or uncomfortable. Maybe he's just cold—or has a big stain on his shirt! If someone's frowning, she might be upset, but she also might be concentrating really hard. Observe some people. Are you able to tell how they feel by watching their body language? Do you think a computer will be able to do that someday?

FUN FACTS

People who use touch screens a lot— **a whole lot!**—sometimes get sore fingertips. So screen makers are using special glass and coatings to prevent this **"finger burn."**

Ever hear of an **interactive wall?** Some projectors have **built-in cameras** to read your gestures, so they **don't need** screens at all.

Through the early 1900s, young students wrote their schoolwork on **small slates.** When they finished their work, it was **wiped clean**—mistakes and all—so they could move to the next assignment. Today, **"wipe the slate clean"** means to **forget past problems** and start something again.

ADDED VALUE

Your teacher can connect an interactive display to a tablet so you can add to the lesson.

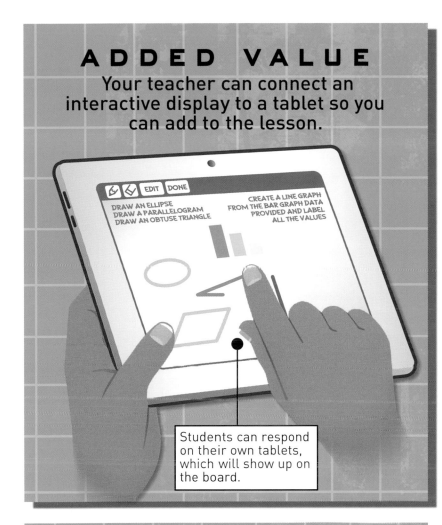

DRAW AN ELLIPSE
DRAW A PARALLELOGRAM
DRAW AN OBTUSE TRIANGLE

CREATE A LINE GRAPH FROM THE BAR GRAPH DATA PROVIDED AND LABEL ALL THE VALUES

Students can respond on their own tablets, which will show up on the board.

PAYING ATTENTION?

Your teacher can make a quiz pop up on your tablet during the lesson.

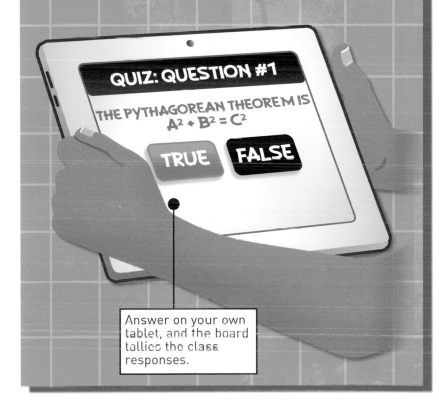

QUIZ: QUESTION #1

THE PYTHAGOREAN THEOREM IS
$A^2 + B^2 = C^2$

TRUE FALSE

Answer on your own tablet, and the board tallies the class responses.

How Things Worked

Way back in the Dark Ages—you know, when your parents were kids—teachers couldn't display lessons on fancy boards by tapping their computers. From the 1800s to the late 1900s, teachers wrote their lessons on chalkboards, or "blackboards," made of smooth pieces of black slate or, later, of man-made materials. And what did you use on a chalkboard? Another rock: chalk. This stuff has been around so long, prehistoric people used it to make cave drawings! Using chalkboards was cheap and easy, but also messy. Chalk dust covered your hands and clothes and drifted through the air. Chalk makers hardened the chalk or coated it to decrease the dust. But they couldn't get rid of those annoying screeches that made students cringe. Dry-erase whiteboards, which started appearing in schools in the 1980s, were a big improvement. Whiteboards had a special coating that let you write on

16mm films were all the rage in the mid-20th century.

them with dry-erase markers. But what if you needed to see something other than words? In the early 1960s, overhead projectors opened up lots of possibilities. These big, boxy contraptions let teachers show entire lessons—words, still pictures, diagrams, maps—on a screen or wall. Teachers wrote or photocopied information onto thin plastic sheets, which they placed on the projector's glass top. A bright light inside the base shone through the plastic sheet and up to an attached mirror, which projected the image. By the 1980s, videocassette recorders, which played tapes on televisions, and, a decade later, DVD players made showing videos and movies much easier. But nothing gets students into their lessons as much as an interactive display!

STICKY SITUATION

How does GLUE stick?

Check It Out!

The glue stick you use to make posters for school may do a lousy job of fixing a broken mug. Different jobs require different types of glue. Some dry faster, some dry stronger. Some are solid, some are runny. Some even have to be heated until they melt to work. But when it comes to sticking things together, they have a lot in common. Stick around to find out why.

What does it take to hold things together?

Why doesn't glue get stuck inside its bottle?

Why does glue dry up?

JUST THE FACTS

Stuck Up

Have you ever seen the picture of a construction worker hanging on a hard hat glued to a beam? It's an amazing sight, and it's thanks to two forces (and really strong glue—don't try it at home!). The glue sticks to the hat and to the beam thanks to a force called adhesion. But that's not the only thing sticking together. The glue also holds itself together with a force called cohesion. It takes both forces to glue two things together. If the glue couldn't hold itself together, it wouldn't matter how well it stuck to the hat or the beam. The glue would just break apart, and the construction worker would fall to the ground. Ouch!

Super Glue's logo comes from an actual contest in which super glue was used to **HOLD UP A CAR!**

IT'S NOT JUST FOR PAPER
Glue can help you transform a stack of toothpicks into something amazing. You add the imagination. The glue will do the rest.

FACTS THAT STICK WITH YOU

We bet glue is **a lot cooler** than you expected, huh? Well, things are about to get even more interesting. Just take a look at some of these **attractive numbers!**

Just **1 SQUARE INCH** (6.5 sq cm) of **SUPER GLUE CAN HOLD** more than **1 TON** (907 kg).

For every person in America, about **40 POUNDS** (18.2 kg) of glue is used on average each year. That's more than **12.5 BILLION POUNDS** (5.7 billion kg) total!

The oldest glue in the world, discovered in Israel, was used more than **8,000 YEARS AGO.**

TELL ME MORE

Why doesn't glue get stuck inside its container? The short answer is, that's the way glue is made. It can't stick until it's out in the air. Inside the bottle or tube, it has water (or chemicals) that keep it fluid, or a bit liquidy.

When you squeeze it out, the water starts to evaporate into the air and the glue starts to dry. It's made that way on purpose, so the glue can do its job. If you forget to put the cap back on, the glue's open to the air—and you know what happens then.

KEEPING IT TOGETHER

Glue relies on some scientific forces to keep your structure together.

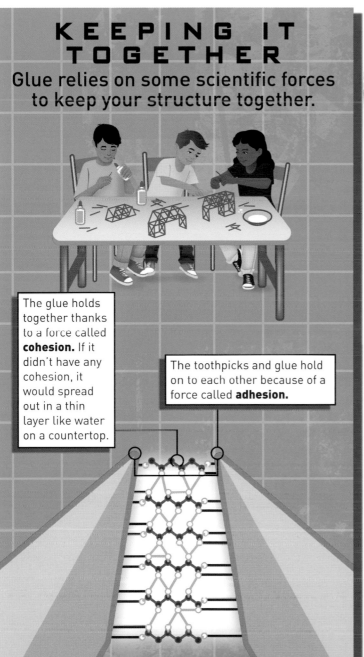

The glue holds together thanks to a force called **cohesion.** If it didn't have any cohesion, it would spread out in a thin layer like water on a countertop.

The toothpicks and glue hold on to each other because of a force called **adhesion.**

Kragle

● In *The LEGO Movie,* **the villain** Lord Business used a powerful weapon called **Kragle** to freeze things in place. Kragle was actually a tube of **Krazy Glue** with some letters rubbed off.

● In **ancient times,** people boiled sugar or **animal parts** in water to make glue. The sticky resin in **pine trees** also became a popular adhesive.

TRY THIS!

Feeling hungry? Fix yourself a peanut butter and jelly sandwich, but don't gobble it up right away. Scoop up a spoonful of jelly. It's sitting in a mound on your spoon, right? Your jelly holds together thanks to a force called cohesion. The same goes for peanut butter. If jelly and peanut butter didn't have any cohesion, they'd sop your bread and slop all over the counter like spilled water. Now spread the jelly and peanut butter on your bread, and put your PB&J together. The peanut butter clings to the jelly—and, on its other side, to the bread—because of a force called adhesion. The same goes for the jelly side.

TALES FROM THE LAB

AN IDEA THAT STUCK:
THE INVENTION OF POST-IT NOTES

The assignment was simple: develop a new adhesive, one with super sticking power.

Spencer Silver, a chemist at the 3M company, was on it. He experimented with different formulas, changing the mix of ingredients to see what would happen. One ingredient started a chemical reaction. Spencer wondered what would happen if he added more of it.

He tried it. "The result was quite astonishing," he said. He was onto something.

He kept working on his discovery. In 1968, he developed an adhesive unlike anything 3M had ever made.

"I CAN STILL FEEL THE EXCITEMENT. I HAD MY PRODUCT: A STICKY NOTE."

It stuck fast but peeled off easily and could be used over and over again.

Spencer was excited about his discovery, but it wasn't what 3M was looking for.

"At that time we wanted to develop bigger, stronger, tougher adhesives," he said. "This was none of those."

WORTH THE WAIT

Spencer didn't give up. For years, he taught groups of 3M scientists about his discovery. One of those scientists was Art Fry, whose job was to dream up new products for 3M to sell. Art thought the new adhesive was interesting, but even he couldn't think of any way to use it.

That is, until he got really frustrated one evening in 1974 while practicing with his church choir. "My bookmark would always fall out, making me lose my place," he said. "I needed one that would stick but not so hard that it would damage the book."

Spencer's adhesive! The next day, Art got some and made a bookmark. He showed it around 3M, but nobody was as excited about it as he was.

One day, Art needed to send his boss a report, but he also had a question for his boss. He didn't want to scribble it on the report itself. How about one of his bookmarks? He cut off a bit, wrote his question on it, and slapped it on the report. His boss answered the same way.

"It was a eureka, head-slapping moment," Art recalled. "I can still feel the excitement. I had my product: a sticky note."

In 1980, Post-it notes went on sale. They became a hit. Today, 3M makes about 50 billion of the notes each year and sells them in more than 150 countries throughout the world.

SPANISH MURALIST IN 2012 CREATED A STOP-MOTION VIDEO AND MURAL IN MADRID, SPAIN, BY SWITCHING OUT MORE THAN POST-IT NOTES.

AT FIRST, POST-IT NOTES CAME **ONLY IN YELLOW.** THE REASON? A LAB NEXT DOOR PROVIDED ITS STOCK OF YELLOW PAPER SCRAPS. THE COLOR STUCK.

STICKY NOTES WERE FIRST CALLED PRESS 'N PEEL. 3M STARTED SELLING THEM IN FOUR STATES, BUT NOT MANY PEOPLE BOUGHT THEM. 3M THEN GAVE A BUNCH AWAY IN BOISE, IDAHO, U.S.A.—WHAT THE COMPANY CALLS THE BOISE BLITZ—AND THE PRODUCT WAS A HIT.

3M GOT ITS START IN **1902** AS THE **MINNESOTA MINING** AND **MANUFACTURING CO.** AT THE TIME, THE COMPANY JUST WANTED TO DIG UP CORUNDUM, A STRONG MINERAL THAT SOMETIMES FORMS **RUBIES** AND **SAPPHIRES.** IT FAILED AS A MINING COMPANY AND HAD TO TRY OTHER THINGS. NOW IT MAKES **60,000** PRODUCTS. ITS FIRST STICKY PRODUCT WAS MASKING TAPE, INVENTED IN 1925.

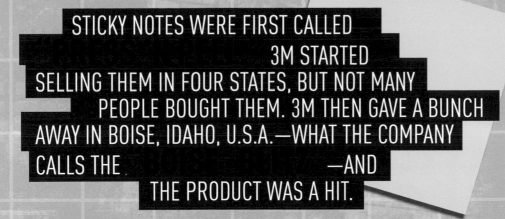

A 2010 NEW YORK ART EXHIBIT SHOWCASED STUDENT ART MADE WITH POST-IT NOTES. ARTISTS USED MORE THAN 100,000 OF THE STICKY NOTES.

This piece of Post-it art used 112,640 sticky notes.

Make It BETTER!

Sticky notes may have gotten off to a rocky start, but nowadays it'd be hard to imagine life without them. And not only are they everywhere, but sticky notes also come in a wide assortment of shapes, sizes, and colors. You can find everything from slender tabs to mark your book pages to huge sticky note tablets for presentations. Want some color? You've got the whole rainbow to choose from.

Plus, you can buy sticky notes in a ton of different shapes, including arrows, puzzle pieces, and animals. It's no wonder some people have made entire murals and artworks out of sticky notes alone!

Now it's your turn to be the inventor. If you designed a new kind of sticky note, what would you improve? What could it do that an average sticky note couldn't?

Grab a pencil and a piece of paper and sketch your ideas. Who knows—your design could be the next big thing in sticky note technology!

COPYCAT

How does a PHOTOCOPIER make copies?

Check It Out!

Clacking and whirring and spitting out paper, a photocopier labors endlessly, copying page after page after page. It's the go-to place when your teacher wants to give you more homework. How can a photocopier make so many math sheets? Does it get tired? Will it ever stop? Find out what a photocopier goes through to multiply your homework.

How does it know how many copies to make ?

Why does it flash that bright light ?

How does the ink get stuck on the page ?

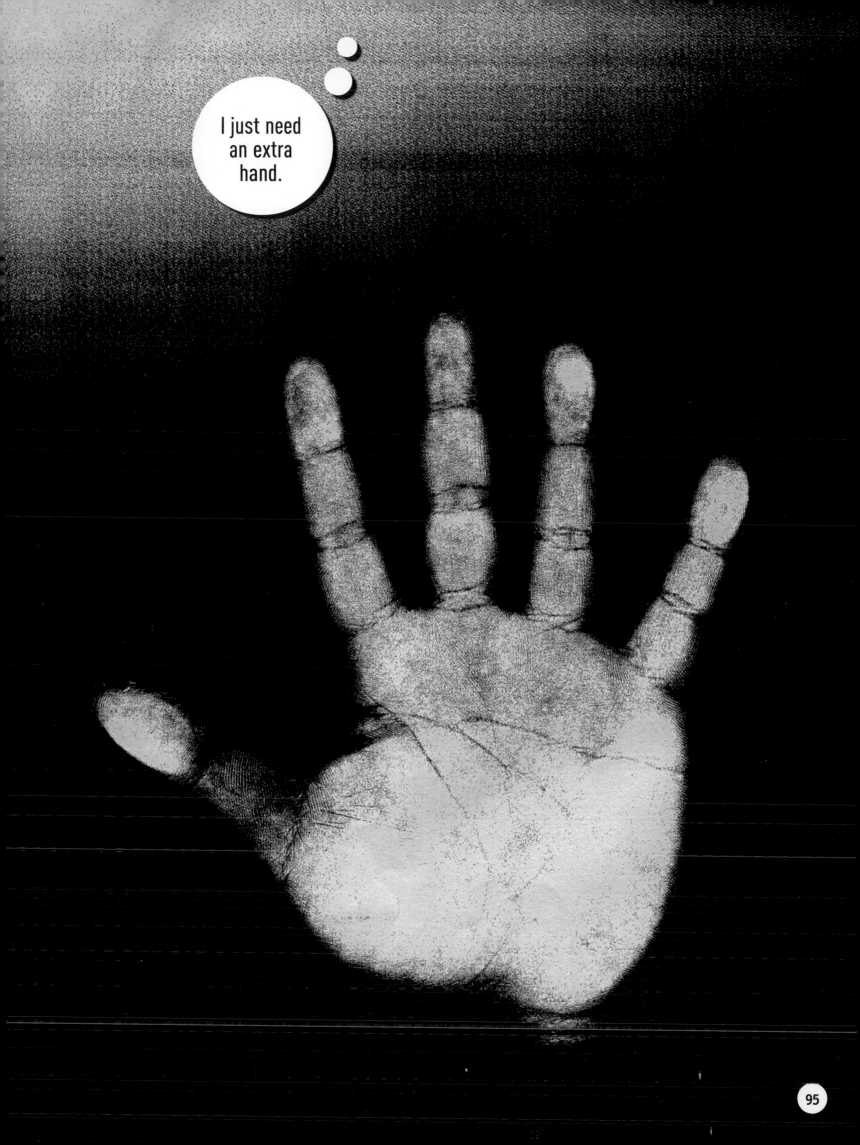

JUST THE FACTS

Copier Tricks

It takes only a few minutes for your teacher to make a stack of math sheets for your entire class. She takes one math sheet and places it problem-side-down on the copier's glass or sets it on a tray that feeds it to the copier. She punches in the number of copies, enough to entertain you and your classmates for hours. Then, with a wicked little cackle (actually, we're just making that up), she presses the start button. A bright light flashes, scanning the math sheet. The white areas of the paper bounce light back onto a special drum inside the photocopier, but the dark areas—all the numbers and words—don't reflect the light. The reflected light creates an image on the drum. Toner (like powdered black ink) sticks to the dark areas—the areas where the light didn't reflect—on the drum. It makes an inked copy of the math sheet, which transfers to a sheet of clean paper that arrives from the paper tray. It does it over and over again, and out come enough math sheets for you and all your classmates.

When **CHESTER CARLSON,** the inventor of photocopying, tried to sell his idea to big companies, they weren't interested. It took him years to find a company to develop his idea.

Getting a Rainbow

Sometimes black and white just isn't enough. If you have a colorful picture, what do you do? You're in luck. Many photocopiers can copy one of those, too. Color photocopiers are like four photocopiers in one. One part handles black, and three others handle colors: cyan, magenta, and yellow. They mix together to create every color in a picture. How do they know what to print? When the bright light scans a color image, the reflected light goes through several filters. Each filter only lets one color through. You end up with four versions of the image in different colors. Sometimes each color goes on a separate drum. Other times, they take turns using one drum. When the paper comes through, it gets toner contact four times, with the toners combining to cover the entire rainbow.

PAPER FOREST

Do you ever feel as if there's a **whole tree's worth** of paper crumpled up at the bottom of your backpack? You might be onto something. Classrooms have started using so much paper that some people are calling for paperless classrooms—where students use laptops and tablets instead. For reference, imagine all the paper you use in a school year. Now imagine how much paper every other student in your school must use, combined. What about the whole world? Whew! That's a lot of paper!

The average school with 100 teachers uses about

250,000 pieces of paper annually.

That's the amount of paper in more than

30 trees!

INNER WORKINGS

A lot goes on behind the scenes to copy the script for your class play.

1. LID/FEEDER:
Your teacher places the original script on the copier's glass or on a tray that feeds it to the copier.

3. LIGHT:
A bright light scans the original paper. The white areas of the paper bounce light onto the drum. The dark areas, like words and numbers, don't reflect the light.

4. DRUM:
The reflected light makes a pattern, like a bright shadow of the original script, on the drum.

2. CONTROL PANEL:
She uses a control panel to tell the photocopier how many copies to make, what they should look like, and when to start working.

5. PAPER:
A clean sheet of paper is pulled out of the paper tray toward the drum.

7. PAPER MEETS DRUM:
The drum transfers the toner onto the sheet of paper. Now your play is on a new sheet of paper.

6. TONER:
Toner attaches to the dark areas on the drum and makes an inked copy of the original script.

8. PAPER EMERGING:
The copy travels to the side of the photocopier and shoots out into a tray.

FUN FACT
SOON AFTER PHOTOCOPIERS CAME OUT, ARTIST BARBARA T. SMITH WAS **SO EXCITED** ABOUT POSSIBLE USES IN HER ART THAT SHE BOUGHT ONE OF THE MACHINES, WHICH WERE **650 POUNDS** (295 KG) AT THE TIME, AND HAD IT INSTALLED IN HER DINING ROOM.

WANT TO KNOW MORE?

TELL ME MORE

GET A CHARGE OUT OF THIS

Just because it's copying your homework doesn't mean a photocopier lacks smarts. It has sophisticated technology inside. It uses static electricity to give things an electrical charge so they stick together—like when you rub a balloon on your hair to get it to stand up. It also uses photoconductivity to capture an image as a pattern of static electricity. As soon as your teacher presses the "start" button, the photocopier prepares the drum inside by giving it an electrical charge. When the bright light scans your teacher's original math sheet, white areas reflect light on the drum, but dark areas do not. The drum is coated with a photoconductive material, and it captures the image—more like a shadow of the math sheet—in a pattern of electrical charges. Where there is light, the photoconductor is discharged. Where it's dark, there is an electrical charge. The black toner gets an opposite electrical charge, so it sticks to the image on the drum. The paper is then placed in contact with the drum and toner. And do you know what makes the toner stick to the paper? Yes, more static electricity, which pulls the paper into the toner. You aced that quiz!

TRY THIS!

You may have heard that white reflects light and black absorbs it. You can test this idea yourself. Take a flashlight, two sheets of white paper, and a sheet of black construction paper into a dark room. Put a sheet of white paper on the floor and hold the flashlight over it so it's pointing up. Hold the second sheet of white paper over the flashlight and shine the light on it. How much light bounces back to the paper on the floor? Now try it with the black construction paper on top. Do you see a difference? A photocopier depends on noticing the differences. It uses a bright light to scan whatever you want to copy. By seeing which areas of your original bounce the light back, it can capture an image of it.

FUN FACTS

● **Photocopier** inventor Chester Carlson produced his first copy in 1938 using **yellowish moss spores** and a zinc plate that had been charged with static electricity by rubbing it with a **handkerchief.**

● When you see a word starting with **"photo" (like photoconductor),** it has something to do with **light.** A photograph is an image made by recording light, either electronically or on film.

● Although real **carbon copies** went the way of dodo birds, the expression "carbon copy" lives on. It means **a person or thing that closely resembles another.**

PUTTING SCIENCE TO WORK

See how a photocopier cleverly combines two scientific tricks to do its job.

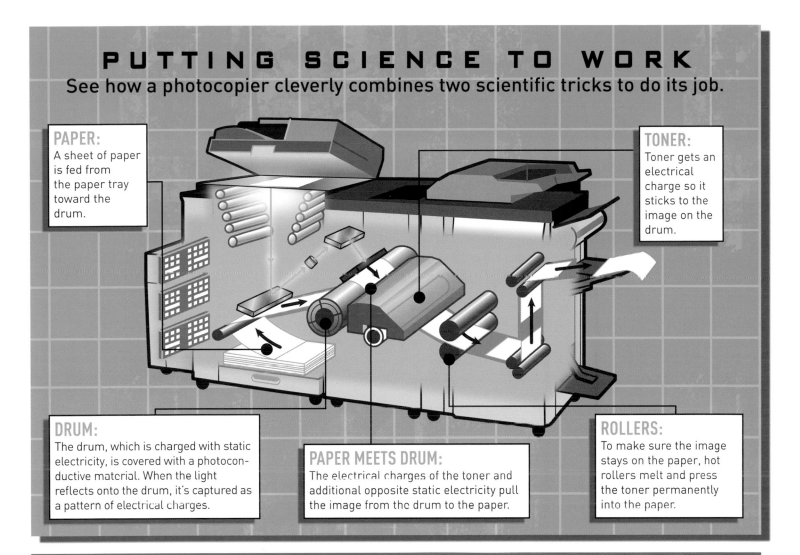

PAPER:
A sheet of paper is fed from the paper tray toward the drum.

TONER:
Toner gets an electrical charge so it sticks to the image on the drum.

DRUM:
The drum, which is charged with static electricity, is covered with a photoconductive material. When the light reflects onto the drum, it's captured as a pattern of electrical charges.

PAPER MEETS DRUM:
The electrical charges of the toner and additional opposite static electricity pull the image from the drum to the paper.

ROLLERS:
To make sure the image stays on the paper, hot rollers melt and press the toner permanently into the paper.

How Things Worked

Ever hear someone say they "cc'd" another person on an email? It means the other person got a copy of the message. But why the extra "c"? To solve that mystery, we need to go back to a time before photocopiers existed. The term "cc" means "carbon copy," and it refers to an old way that people made copies for more than 150 years. They'd sandwich a piece of carbon paper, a tissue-thin paper with waxy ink on one side, between two sheets of regular paper. When they wrote or typed on the top sheet, the carbon paper made an instant copy on the second sheet. Trouble is, you could only make a couple of copies that way. That was fine for businesses, but not for schools. What fun is only a couple of homework sheets?

Between the 1950s and 1970s, teachers cranked out copies of tests or worksheets on mimeograph or Ditto machines. They worked pretty much the same way, but with one big difference. Mimeographs, first available in the late 1880s, used stencils. The worksheet content was cut into the stencil, and the stencil wrapped around a cylinder or drum on the machine. When the cylinder was turned, ink was squeezed through the stencil and onto sheets of paper. The Ditto machine, invented in the 1920s, used something similar to carbon paper, which made a master worksheet in colored wax. Teachers wrapped the master sheet around the cylinder and turned it, leaving waxy ink copies on new sheets of paper. Copies fresh from the Ditto machine were

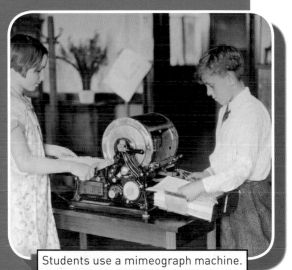

Students use a mimeograph machine.

stinky. They were also purple; that was the color of the waxy ink. Teachers had to crank early mimeograph and Ditto machines by hand, and pouring ink into the machines was a tricky feat that often left their hands covered in purple. Still, it beat making copies by hand!

DOUBLE DUTY

How does a THERMOS keep hot stuff hot and cold things cold?

Check It Out!

Bored of sandwiches? Try bringing some soup or pasta to school for lunch. But how do you keep it from becoming cold and yucky by your lunch period? Pull out your trusty thermos! It's a wonder at keeping hot food and drinks hot (and cold stuff cold). Want to know how it works? Let's find out how a thermos handles heat.

Why is it a lot bigger on the outside than on the inside **?**

How long does it keep things hot or cold **?**

Why's it so hard to keep hot cocoa warm in a mug **?**

JUST THE FACTS

Master Controller

A thermos, or vacuum flask, is a super-insulated container. It has a simple, clever design to keep heat trapped inside—or to prevent heat from getting in. It's like a double-walled container inside a tough outer shell. Between the layers, there's nothing—really! Even the air has been sucked out to create a vacuum. Heat can't cross a vacuum. Sometimes the inside chamber is made of shiny glass, which could break with a bad drop. But many thermoses use two layers of stainless steel with a reflecting layer and vacuum between them. The shiny surfaces and reflecting layer bounce back any heat that tries to pass. The top lid is designed to fit tightly so nothing, including heat, can get out.

The Thermos company, the first to sell **VACUUM FLASKS,** did a really good job of making the word "thermos" popular—maybe **TOO GOOD.** A court ruled in 1963 that "thermos" had become a general description. People could use it to refer to any vacuum flask, even if it wasn't made by Thermos.

TRY THIS!

Do you think you can make a bottle that insulates as well as a thermos? Find several jars and try to insulate them with different materials, like newspaper, foam, or aluminum foil. Which works best? How do they stack up to a thermos? Do you feel any heat escaping? How would you stop that? (Tip: Don't use a food that spoils fast or superhot liquids that could burn you. Better safe than sorry!)

OLYMPIC SLURPERS

Even if you don't bring a thermos to school, a lot of other kids **probably do.** Just check out how much soup is consumed **per year** in the United States. It would take a pretty big thermos to hold all that soup!

Americans eat more than **10 BILLION** BOWLS of soup a year. That's more than **780 MILLION GALLONS.** That amount of soup could fill more than **1,183 OLYMPIC-SIZE SWIMMING POOLS!**

FUN FACT

A THERMOS ISN'T THE ONLY WAY TO **KEEP YOUR LUNCH WARM.** SOME COMPANIES MAKE **INSULATED LUNCH BOXES** THAT PLUG INTO A COMPUTER TO STAY TOASTY.

Every part of a thermos works to prevent heat from getting out (or in, if you're trying to keep the contents cold). The shiny, mirrored lining inside reflects heat back where it came from so it can't leave in a process called radiation. The tight lid prevents air from entering or leaving the thermos, so heat can't rise, only to be replaced by cooler air, a process called convection. Finally, the vacuum between layers prevents conduction, which is when heat travels to a cooler thing that it's touching. With all those parts working together, your food or drink stays at just the right temperature for hours.

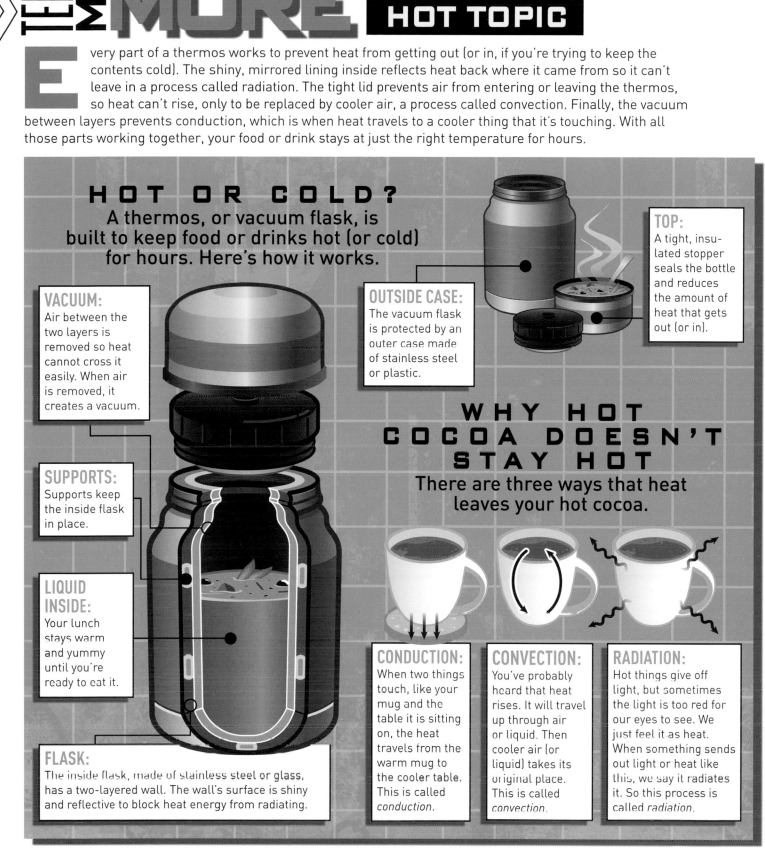

HOT OR COLD?

A thermos, or vacuum flask, is built to keep food or drinks hot (or cold) for hours. Here's how it works.

TOP:
A tight, insulated stopper seals the bottle and reduces the amount of heat that gets out (or in).

OUTSIDE CASE:
The vacuum flask is protected by an outer case made of stainless steel or plastic.

VACUUM:
Air between the two layers is removed so heat cannot cross it easily. When air is removed, it creates a vacuum.

SUPPORTS:
Supports keep the inside flask in place.

LIQUID INSIDE:
Your lunch stays warm and yummy until you're ready to eat it.

FLASK:
The inside flask, made of stainless steel or glass, has a two-layered wall. The wall's surface is shiny and reflective to block heat energy from radiating.

WHY HOT COCOA DOESN'T STAY HOT

There are three ways that heat leaves your hot cocoa.

CONDUCTION:
When two things touch, like your mug and the table it is sitting on, the heat travels from the warm mug to the cooler table. This is called *conduction*.

CONVECTION:
You've probably heard that heat rises. It will travel up through air or liquid. Then cooler air (or liquid) takes its original place. This is called *convection*.

RADIATION:
Hot things give off light, but sometimes the light is too red for our eyes to see. We just feel it as heat. When something sends out light or heat like this, we say it radiates it. So this process is called *radiation*.

● Scottish scientist **Sir James Dewar** studied objects at extremely **low temperatures,** but he couldn't keep the gases cold long enough. So, in 1892, he invented the **vacuum flask.** Unfortunately, he didn't patent his invention. Scientists still refer to a thermos as a "Dewar flask" in his honor.

FUN FACT

STRIKE UP THE BAND

How do MUSICAL INSTRUMENTS make so many sounds?

Check It Out!

It's music class! Time to get your groove on. Grab an instrument and get down with some serious science. Yes, science. There's more to making music than banging, plucking, or blowing air through an instrument. Let's strike up the band to find out how.

How do instruments make so many different sounds?

Why do piccolos play higher notes than flutes?

Why does my friend's guitar sound different from mine?

JUST THE FACTS

Good Vibes

Musical instruments come in all shapes and sizes, but they have one thing in common. They make music when something on them vibrates, shaking back and forth really fast. It could be a string, a tube filled with air, a drumhead, or even something solid like a hunk of wood. When you pluck it, blow through it, or hit it with a drumstick (not the chicken kind), the vibrations take off, spreading out and traveling as sound waves to your ears. The next thing you know, you're rocking out to your favorite tunes.

35,000-year-old bone flute found west of Ulm, Germany

Some **ARCHAEOLOGISTS** think music may have helped Homo sapiens, the first modern humans, **FORM BIGGER SOCIETIES.**

Key Concern

If all musical instruments make sound by vibrating, why do they sound so different? The design of the instrument is key. Its size and shape, what it's made of, what vibrates on it, and how it's played all affect its sound. Even two guitars might sound a lot different depending on the kind of wood used to make them or what their strings are made of. Add to that the different skills and styles of musicians, and you've got a unique sound.

Violins can produce many different kinds of sounds.

STRUMMING AROUND THE WORLD

Instruments have been around for about as long as human culture has. And like cultures, instruments are hugely diverse. The funny thing is, though, no matter how creative and cool an instrument is, someone is probably already playing something similar to it on the other side of the world! Take a look at how different cultures filled their need for rhythm with these variations on the plucking instrument (aka the guitar!).

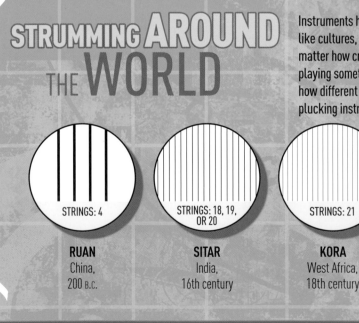

STRINGS: 4	STRINGS: 18, 19, OR 20	STRINGS: 21	STRINGS: 6	STRINGS: 3 OR 4
RUAN China, 200 B.C.	**SITAR** India, 16th century	**KORA** West Africa, 18th century	**MODERN CLASSICAL GUITAR** Spain, 19th century	**APPALACHIAN DULCIMER** United States, 19th century

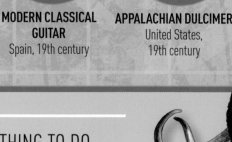

FUN FACT

EVER HEAR OF **ORGANOLOGY?** IT HAS NOTHING TO DO WITH YOUR INTERNAL ORGANS. IT'S THE **SCIENCE OF MUSICAL INSTRUMENTS.**

MUSIC MAKERS

You make sound by getting something on an instrument to vibrate.
Instruments are grouped in a family when they make sound in a similar way.

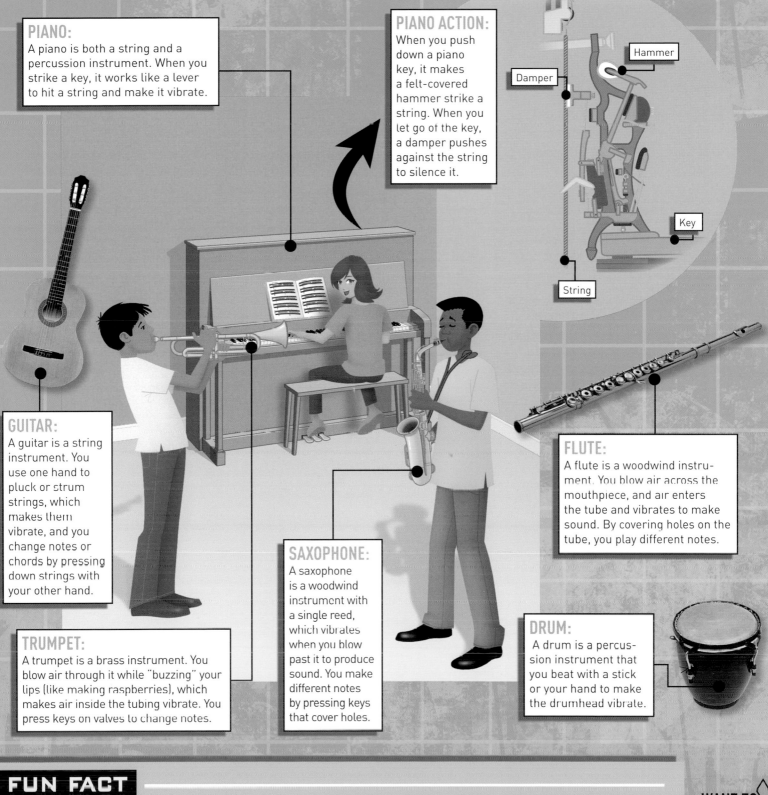

PIANO:
A piano is both a string and a percussion instrument. When you strike a key, it works like a lever to hit a string and make it vibrate.

PIANO ACTION:
When you push down a piano key, it makes a felt-covered hammer strike a string. When you let go of the key, a damper pushes against the string to silence it.

Hammer

Damper

Key

String

GUITAR:
A guitar is a string instrument. You use one hand to pluck or strum strings, which makes them vibrate, and you change notes or chords by pressing down strings with your other hand.

TRUMPET:
A trumpet is a brass instrument. You blow air through it while "buzzing" your lips (like making raspberries), which makes air inside the tubing vibrate. You press keys on valves to change notes.

SAXOPHONE:
A saxophone is a woodwind instrument with a single reed, which vibrates when you blow past it to produce sound. You make different notes by pressing keys that cover holes.

FLUTE:
A flute is a woodwind instrument. You blow air across the mouthpiece, and air enters the tube and vibrates to make sound. By covering holes on the tube, you play different notes.

DRUM:
A drum is a percussion instrument that you beat with a stick or your hand to make the drumhead vibrate.

FUN FACT
THE **OLDEST KNOWN** MUSICAL INSTRUMENTS ARE FLUTES MADE OF BIRD BONES AND MAMMOTH IVORY. FOUND IN CAVES IN SOUTHWESTERN GERMANY, THESE FLUTES ARE BELIEVED TO BE **42,000 TO 43,000** YEARS OLD.

WANT TO
KNOW
MORE?

TELL ME MORE!

CATCHY TUNES

Sound waves are contagious. When something on your musical instrument vibrates, it makes ripples in the air around it. The ripples, or sound waves, act differently depending on how loud or soft a sound is (its volume) or how high or low it is (its pitch). Big booms travel on tall waves, while whispers have short peaks. A sound's pitch depends on how fast the waves vibrate. Low sounds vibrate slowly. It takes a large instrument to make them. But high-pitched sounds vibrate more frequently and come from smaller instruments. Picture it this way: The waves are squeezed inside a smaller space, so they bounce around faster.

NOTE THIS!

If you play a musical instrument, you already know how to play different notes. You push keys, press down strings, or strike different parts of the instrument. What you're actually doing is changing the size of what vibrates. On a stringed instrument, pressing the string against the wooden neck makes the string's vibrating length shorter. It makes a higher note, like it's suddenly a smaller instrument. When you cover holes on a wind instrument like a flute, you give the air inside more room to vibrate. It's like you made a longer instrument, and it plays a lower note. Thicker strings or longer xylophone bars do the same thing.

MIXING IT UP

A musical instrument doesn't make just one sound wave at a time. It sends out a whole mix of different waves. The mixture gives the musical note a special quality, called timbre.

TRY THIS!

Reed instruments, such as saxophones and clarinets, use a thin strip of wood or plastic to make sounds when you blow over it. You can make a reed out of—you guessed it—a reed of grass. Pick the thickest, flattest blade you can find. Hold the bottom flat and tightly between the heels of your hands at the base of your thumbs. Bend your thumbs a teeny bit and press them together to hold the top of the reed. Blow between the knuckles and bottoms of your thumbs, and you should get a loud squeak. If it doesn't work, move your thumbs up or down a little to hold the reed tighter or give it more room to vibrate. Like all music, it takes practice!

FUN FACTS

Luray Caverns Organ

- Luray Caverns, **a massive cave** in Virginia, U.S.A., has an organ made out of stalactites, the limestone rock formations that hang from the cave's ceiling. Mathematician and scientist Leland Sprinkle got the idea to **build it in 1954** after a tour guide at the caverns tapped a stalactite and it sounded awesome. It took Sprinkle **3 years** to make the organ, which spreads over 3.5 acres (1.4 ha) of the cave.

- Cows produce **more milk** when they listen to **relaxing music.**

GETTING A BIG SOUND

An instrument's shape affects its sound's loudness and quality.

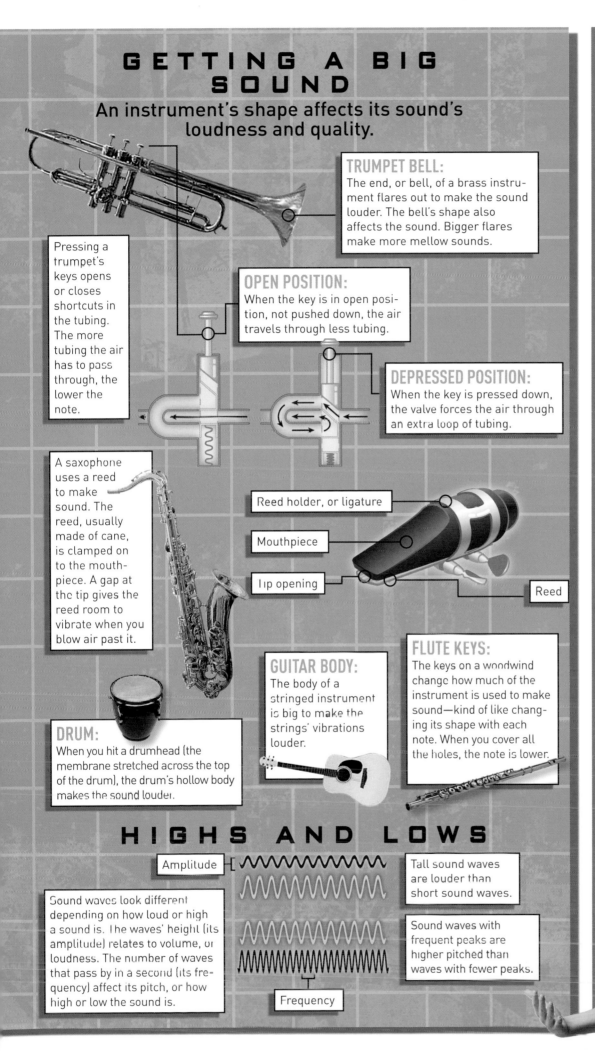

TRUMPET BELL:
The end, or bell, of a brass instrument flares out to make the sound louder. The bell's shape also affects the sound. Bigger flares make more mellow sounds.

Pressing a trumpet's keys opens or closes shortcuts in the tubing. The more tubing the air has to pass through, the lower the note.

OPEN POSITION:
When the key is in open position, not pushed down, the air travels through less tubing.

DEPRESSED POSITION:
When the key is pressed down, the valve forces the air through an extra loop of tubing.

A saxophone uses a reed to make sound. The reed, usually made of cane, is clamped on to the mouthpiece. A gap at the tip gives the reed room to vibrate when you blow air past it.

Reed holder, or ligature

Mouthpiece

Tip opening

Reed

GUITAR BODY:
The body of a stringed instrument is big to make the strings' vibrations louder.

FLUTE KEYS:
The keys on a woodwind change how much of the instrument is used to make sound—kind of like changing its shape with each note. When you cover all the holes, the note is lower.

DRUM:
When you hit a drumhead (the membrane stretched across the top of the drum), the drum's hollow body makes the sound louder.

HIGHS AND LOWS

Amplitude

Tall sound waves are louder than short sound waves.

Sound waves look different depending on how loud or high a sound is. The waves' height (its amplitude) relates to volume, or loudness. The number of waves that pass by in a second (its frequency) affect its pitch, or how high or low the sound is.

Sound waves with frequent peaks are higher pitched than waves with fewer peaks.

Frequency

PROFILE: Nicolás "Cola" Gómez

RECYCLERS, INNOVATORS, MUSIC MAKERS

On the far outskirts of the capital of Paraguay, a trash dump stretches for blocks. Families living nearby pick through the muck for stuff to sell. But one garbage picker searches for something else, junk that can become a thing of beauty.

That man is Nicolás "Cola" Gómez. He's been a *ganchero*, a professional garbage picker, for years. But now Cola has a new job. He's a luthier, someone who makes stringed musical instruments. He makes them out of trash. And he makes them for a symphony orchestra.

> **"THESE INSTRUMENTS DON'T HAVE ANY MONETARY VALUE. THEY ONLY HAVE VALUE WHEN THEY'RE IN THE HANDS OF THE CHILDREN PLAYING THE MUSIC."**

The Recycled Orchestra is made up of a group of children who live near the dump in Cateura, one of the poorest areas in Latin America. The group has toured the world giving concerts on instruments made from oil drums, wood pallets, baking sheets, tin cans, bottle caps, and other junk people have thrown away.

"The world sends us garbage. We send back music," says Favio Chávez, the music teacher who started the orchestra.

TRASH TO TREASURE

In 2006, Favio was an environmental technician working on a recycling program in Cateura. He was horrified to see children playing at the dump. He wanted to do something about it. But what?

Music was the first thing that had given Favio a sense of purpose. He thought it might help the children of Cateura, too. He offered free music lessons. Dozens of kids signed up—so many that he needed more instruments.

But there was a problem.

"A community like Cateura is not a place to have a violin," Favio says. "In fact, a violin is worth more than a house here." Houses in Cateura are built of junk from the dump.

But that gave Favio an idea. Could they make instruments from recycled materials?

"Favio brought me a violin as a model," Cola says. Cola used to be a carpenter and wanted to help the kids, too. "I made my calculations and looked for an aluminum can. I prepared it, I put the neck and cords on it."

Cola hammered out the shape until he transformed the trash into a musical instrument. "It was a continuous process of trial and error," he says.

It looked pretty rough, but it sounded sweet. It was perfect.

"These instruments don't have any monetary value. They can't be sold. They can't be pawned. They can't be stolen," Favio says. "They only have value when they're in the hands of the children playing the music."

And play they do—really, really well. Some orchestra members have become professional musicians, and others were invited to the United States to study. For the first time, the kids see a future away from Cateura, away from the landfill.

As for the orchestra itself, it plays world-class music, the same pieces performed by top symphony orchestras around the world. Favio leads them on a guitar Cola made from two metal tins.

RECYCLED ORCHESTRA MEMBERS PLAYED WITH THRASH METAL BAND DURING A 2013 CONCERT IN THE UNITED STATES AND OPENED FOR DURING A 2014 SOUTH AMERICAN TOUR.

and Favio Chávez

A FULL-LENGTH DOCUMENTARY MOVIE, *LANDFILL HARMONIC,* TELLS THE STORY OF THE RECYCLED ORCHESTRA. THE MOVIE'S TRAILER **WENT VIRAL** ON THE INTERNET.

THE RECYCLED ORCHESTRA CAN PLAY MANY TYPES OF MUSIC—
CLASSICAL, PARAGUAYAN FOLK TUNES, BEATLES SONGS, JAZZ, OR **HEAVY METAL.**

DO-OVER

How do ERASERS make your mistakes disappear?

Check It Out!

Everyone makes mistakes. Sometimes they even help you figure out a better way to do something. But other times you want to get rid of them. Like on a spelling test—definitely not the best time for a mistake. Or when you're putting the final touches on a great piece of art. You know what to do: Grab an eraser. No mistake about it, erasers are clever little tools that help make us look good. Find out how they get rid of your mistakes.

What's all that little stuff the eraser leaves on my paper **?**

Why won't my eraser work with my favorite pen **?**

Why isn't my erasable ink erasable anymore **?**

JUST THE FACTS

The Graphic Details

The "lead" in a pencil is really a mineral called graphite. When you write with a pencil, you leave little pieces of graphite stuck to the fibers in the paper. Erasers pick up the graphite, removing it from the surface of the paper. It's not as easy as it sounds. When you rub an eraser across a pencil mark, a couple of things happen. Abrasives in the eraser (rough things like pumice) gently scratch the paper's surface to loosen the graphite. Sticky parts of the eraser grab and hold on to the graphite bits. Then they crumble off onto your paper, waiting for you to blow or brush them away.

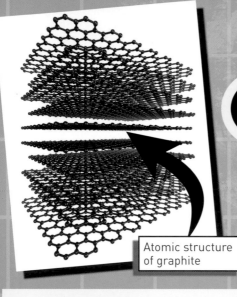

Atomic structure of graphite

Rubbing It In

Friction helps erasers work. Friction, which happens when two things rub against each, creates heat. (That's why you can warm up your hands by rubbing them together.) In an eraser, the heat makes the rubber stickier, so it's easier for it to grab and hold on to the graphite bits.

Legend has it that English engineer Edward Nairne invented the eraser in 1770 **BY MISTAKE**. He accidentally grabbed a hunk of rubber. It worked. He started selling rubber erasers. He was reaching for a wad of bread to erase a mistake (yes, really—that's what they used back then), but he grabbed a hunk of rubber instead.

PENCIL PUSHING

We use a lot of pencils in the world. And a lot of graphite (not lead!) and wood is needed to make all those pencils. And with that much writing going on, we're bound to make mistakes—it's only natural. Good thing we've got plenty of erasers!

You could circle the **EARTH** more than **40 TIMES** with the number of pencils produced in 2004 alone, and that only includes the ones made in China!

FUN FACT

SOME PEOPLE THINK **"RUBBER ERASER"** REFERS TO WHAT THE ERASER IS MADE OF. OTHERS THINK IT REFERS TO HOW YOU USE IT—BY RUBBING. NO ONE'S SURE WHO'S RIGHT. IT'S ONE OF LIFE'S GREAT **MYSTERIES.**

TACKLING MISTAKES

Pink rubber erasers attack your mistakes in a couple of ways.

The eraser gently scratches the top surface of the paper to loosen the graphite.

The eraser, which is stickier than paper, grabs and lifts the graphite off the paper.

Small pieces of rubber, which are stuck to graphite, remain behind.

Pencil "lead" is made of graphite, a form of carbon. Graphite leaves a darker mark than real lead, but its main advantage is that, unlike lead, it's nontoxic and not harmful to your health.

WHY SO MANY ERASERS?

If you're working on art, you don't want your paper roughed up or pencil graphite smeared across your page. Set aside your pink eraser, as there are better options.

ART GUM ERASER:
Art gum erasers are made of very soft, coarse rubber. They don't rough up the paper, but they leave a lot of crumbles behind.

VINYL ERASER:
Vinyl erasers are made of a soft plastic, but they're very tough. They erase cleanly and completely, but they can tear up the paper if you're not careful.

KNEADED ERASER:
Kneaded erasers are supersoft erasers that feel like putty. They lift graphite (or artist's charcoal) off the paper and hold on to it. They don't wear out, but they eventually get dirty. They also don't hurt the paper.

FUN FACT

THERE'S A GOOD REASON WE MISTAKENLY CALL THE CORE OF A **PENCIL "LEAD."** ANCIENT ROMANS USED A THIN LEAD ROD **CALLED A STYLUS.** LEAD IS A SOFT METAL, SO IT LEAVES MARKS BEHIND.

WANT TO KNOW MORE?

ERASER

THE HARD TRUTH

Erasers contain a softener, kind of like vegetable oil, to prevent them from getting hard and to help keep the paper from tearing when you rub it. (Yeah, it doesn't always work.) The oil doesn't last forever, and so your eraser can dry out, which makes it pretty useless. You can try cutting off the hard parts to get to the softer rubber beneath. If you really want to make your eraser last longer, keep it in an airtight container.

INK GETS INTO THE ACT
Not everyone likes to write with pencils. But how do pen-wielding people get rid of their mistakes? Most can't. Regular ink is made of dyes and oils that leave permanent marks in paper. Rubbing them with an eraser only smears the ink. Don't despair—pen makers have come to the rescue. They've made pens with erasable "ink." Some of it isn't ink at all. It's something like liquid rubber cement, which is colored to look like ink. An eraser can rub it off the paper—but only for a while. After several hours, it hardens and becomes permanent. Another type of erasable ink, called thermochromic ink, is dark only when it's cool. If you rub an eraser over it, you create heat through friction. The heat turns the ink clear, so your mistake disappears. If you've ever used an erasable ink pen, you've probably worked that kind of magic.

TRY THIS!
Before there were rubber erasers, people rubbed away their mistakes using wads of bread. Like erasers, bread is sticky enough to pick up graphite. In fact, some artists still use bread to lighten art charcoal or pastel marks. Give it a try. Take a slice of bread, remove the crusts, and form it into a wad. Rub it over some pencil marks. You can tell your parents it's art. If you're really feeling like a scientist, conduct an experiment to find out which works better, whole wheat bread or white bread.

● In 1858, Hymen Lipman, who ran a **stationery company,** received a patent for attaching erasers to the tops of pencils. **The patent** was later taken back, because he had only combined two things together instead of **inventing something new.**

Pencil + eraser. Not revolutionary, just common sense.

FUN FACTS

● Unlike real lead, graphite is **soft** and **brittle** and needs a holder. The first graphite sticks in the **1500s** were wrapped in string. Later, graphite was stuck into **hollowed-out wooden sticks.**

● In **1564,** a lot of **graphite** was discovered in England. It left a **darker mark** than lead, so the locals used it for marking sheep! Some other people figured it would make **good pencils,** too.

UP CLOSE

If you could put your pink eraser under a strong magnifying glass, you'd see why it's so good at its job. It is rough enough to scratch graphite off paper, and its little pockets increase the amount of surface that can stick to the graphite.

INK THAT REALLY ISN'T

Erasable pens don't use the same kind of ink as a regular pen. In some pens, the "ink" is more like colored liquid rubber cement. In others, it's a heat-sensitive ink that becomes clear when erased.

How Things Worked

As long as people have been writing, they've been making mistakes—and wanting to get rid of them. So what did people do before the invention of the rubber eraser in 1770? In the earliest days of writing, they couldn't do much. The first writing was carved into clay tablets. Once the clay dried, there was no changing it (though it could be smashed). It was a bit easier to deal with mistakes on papyrus and parchment—but only a little bit. Papyrus, invented by the Egyptians 5,000 years ago, was made of thin plant strips layered and pressed together. Parchment, which has been around for more than 2,000 years, was made of animal skin that had been specially treated, scraped, stretched, and dried. Writers may have been able to use a rough stone, like pumice or sandstone, to scrape ink off these materials, especially parchment, and correct small mistakes. More often, they scraped off all the writing or washed the sheet clean with a mixture of milk and oat bran. Papyrus and parchment cost a lot. So people used the materials over and over for years—even centuries! (Using laboratory equipment, scientists can see old layers of writing in books made of parchment.) Parchment and papyrus documents were meant to last. But if people only needed to jot down notes or lessons, they used book-size wax tablets. The

tablets started as a piece of wood and were hollowed out on one side and filled with a thin layer of wax. People used a stylus—a tool made of metal, wood, or bone that was pointy on one end and flat on the other—to write in the wax. It was easy to erase their writing. People either smoothed the wax with the flat end of their stylus, or they heated it up to melt it.

TRY THIS!

MUSIC MASTERS:

MAKE A THINGAMAJIG THAT PLAYS

Get ready to rock. You're going to make a magnificent musical instrument, and we'll show you exactly how to do it! Um, wait a minute, we changed our mind. Music is all about creativity, right? (Yeah, OK—that and skill.) So let's get creative. We're *not* going to give you step-by-step instructions for this one, just some things to think about. And a challenge. All around the world, people build instruments from whatever they can find. Can you?

WHAT YOU NEED

TIME: a few minutes to a few hours (and more to jam)

Ask an adult to help.

1. All kinds of stuff—solid, hollow, wiggly, stretchy, stringy, rattly—that's been thrown away, underused, or not valued for the awesome sound it can make

2. Things like boxes, cookie tins, Styrofoam coolers, cones, and big tubes that can provide a body or structure for your instrument and/or help it sound louder

3. Little parts like screws, keys, or sticks that can hold, lift, and stretch strings and other stretchy stuff

4. Tools and supplies to cut and put things together

5. Imagination

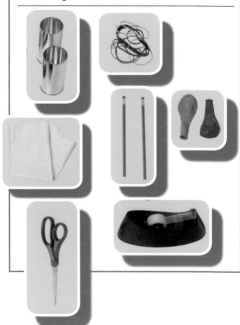

1. DECIDE HOW YOU WANT
to play your instrument. By striking it with your hand, a stick, or your dad's best golf club (not recommended)? Blowing through it? Shaking it? Strumming or plucking it? Dragging something, like a bow or stick, across it? Shaking, rattling, or rolling it?

2. PICK SOMETHING THAT
can do what you've chosen in Step 1—and that makes a cool sound when you do it. Like to pluck? Try strings or rubber bands. Prefer to whack? Find something solid or stretchy for a drumhead. Full of hot air? Go for a tube or bottle. You get the idea.

3. FIGURE OUT IF YOU
need to add a body or something to make your instrument louder. Experiment! Attach strings to a sturdy box of some sort (Styrofoam cooler, cookie tin, wood box) with holes. Add a cone to a horn. Stretch a drumhead (balloon, latex glove) over a big tube. Build a support that holds pipes or wood loosely so they can vibrate when you strike them.

4. COME UP WITH A
way to make different notes. Can you add cans or tubes of different sizes to your instrument? Can you change the length of strings or use your fingers to press them down on something? How about putting finger holes in a tube you blow through?

5. USE DUCT TAPE, SCREWS,
whatever, to keep it together.

6. FEEL FREE TO DECORATE
it—but not on the parts that vibrate.

7. GIVE A CONCERT!

STUCK? If you need inspiration, watch a video of Australian musician Linsey Pollak making a clarinet out of a carrot (yes, a carrot) or check out the websites of Bash the Trash, the New York Philharmonic, and other symphony orchestras. They're listed in the back of this book.

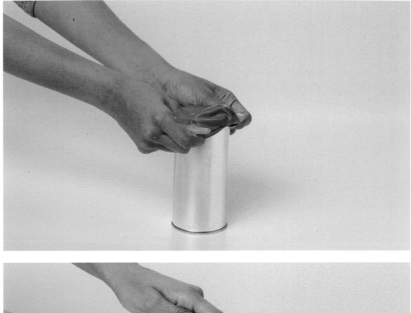

Instruments can be fancy, curly, or curvy contraptions with keys and moving parts, or they can be simple sticks or tubes with holes punched in them. They can be made of brass—or trash. It doesn't matter. The science behind how they work is the same. You have to make something vibrate, or shake back and forth, which sends out sound waves. Bigger instruments generally make lower sounds, and smaller ones make higher sounds. That's why you get different notes—higher or lower—by pushing down on strings or covering up finger holes. It's like changing the instrument's size, because you're using more or less of it to make the music.

CHAPTER 4
EXTREME FUN

There's a little daredevil in all of us.
WE LOVE THRILLS.

We want to jump the highest jump, ride the fastest coaster, and find the next challenge. We imagine ourselves as a surfer riding a towering wave. We picture ourselves on the high wire. We're ready for fast-paced, high-excitement action. And there are plenty of places to find it—from your backyard, to an amusement park, to Mother Nature itself. Prep your inner daredevil and get ready to go to the extreme.

ON A ROLL

Why is a ROLLER COASTER so thrilling?

Check It Out!

Seeking a thrill? You know where to get it: that towering roller coaster rising high above all the other rides in the amusement park. It's a wild ride that's specially designed to push and pull you in different directions and make you feel like you're speeding down the track out of control. So buckle up, and check out how a roller coaster puts science to work.

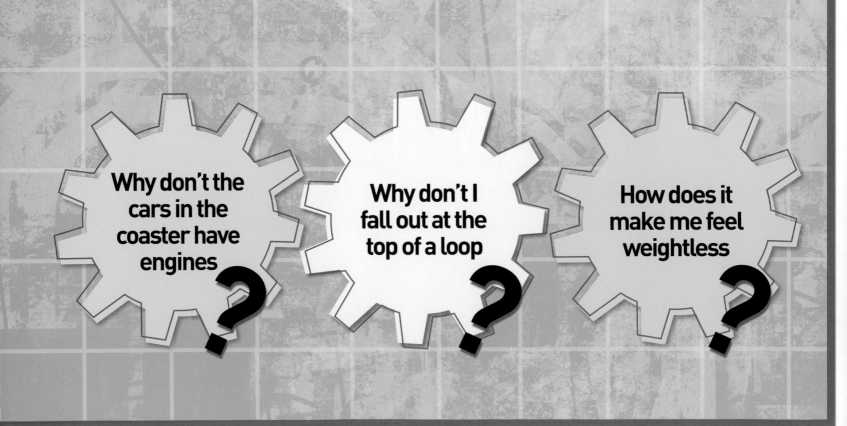

Why don't the cars in the coaster have engines?

Why don't I fall out at the top of a loop?

How does it make me feel weightless?

JUST THE FACTS

Ups and Downs

The excitement builds. You settle into your seat and pull on the safety harness. You coast out of the station like this is just some pleasure ride. But you know it's not. You face the first hill, the one towering above the rest of the track. Your car grabs on to a chain, and you clankety-clank all the way to the top. That's the only time your coaster needs an extra boost. You take off down that first hill, and your train zooms along under its own power. It zips up and down hills, through twists and turns, and around spirals and loop-de-loops. As you head back to the station, brakes built into the track clamp on to the train to bring you to a stop. The ride's over, but the thrill remains.

An Energizing Experience

The ups and downs of a roller-coaster ride are not just thrilling. They're specially designed to power you through your ride. In most coasters, as you climb that first hill— the tallest on the track—you build potential energy, stored up energy that's kind of like fuel for your ride. When you zoom down hills, gravity— the force that holds us to the Earth—is at work. All that potential energy you stored up turns into kinetic energy, the energy of motion, and you fly along the tracks. When the brakes clamp on at the end of your ride, they use friction to slow you down.

BIGGEST HILL:
As the train climbs up the first hill, it also builds up potential energy. The top of the first hill, the highest hill, is also the highest point of potential energy.

CHAIN LIFT:
In most coasters, a chain under the track pulls your train up the first hill. The chain loops around a gear at the top of the hill and another at the bottom, which is run by a motor. The train cars hold on to the chain with special hooks called chain dogs.

BRAKES:
Roller-coaster brakes are built into the tracks, not the coaster cars. The clamps rub against your train, creating friction, and bring you to a gentle stop.

KING COASTER

Kingda Ka at Six Flags Great Adventure in New Jersey, U.S.A., rockets straight up to the height of a 45-story skyscraper. It goes from 0 to 128 miles an hour (206 km/h) in only 3.5 seconds, making it the **fastest coaster** in America. But its speed isn't the only thing that makes this coaster so intense—just take a look these supersize stats.

FUN FACT
CONEY ISLAND'S HISTORIC **CYCLONE COASTER** COST $175,000 TO CONSTRUCT BACK IN 1927. TODAY, IT TAKES SEVERAL MILLION DOLLARS TO BUILD AN AVERAGE COASTER, WITH THE MOST COMPLICATED ONES COSTING AROUND $25 MILLION.

FULL OF POTENTIAL

A roller coaster's ups and downs constantly convert potential energy to kinetic energy and back again. Buckle up to see physics at work.

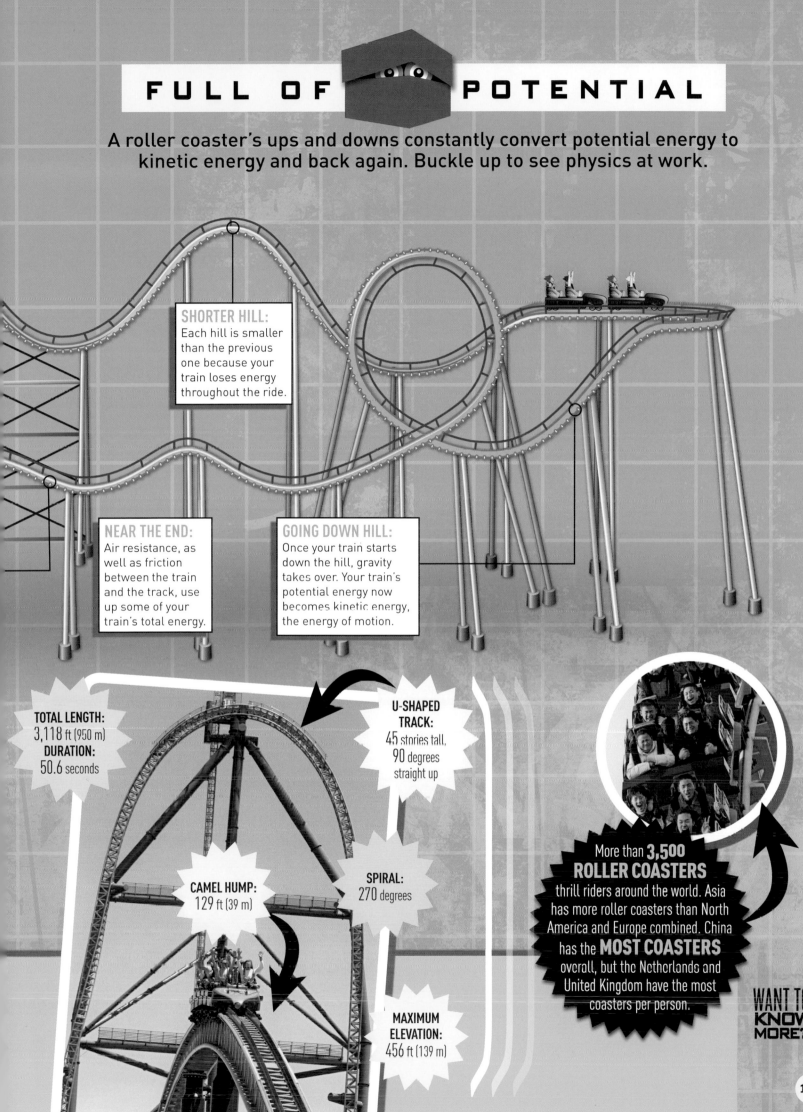

SHORTER HILL:
Each hill is smaller than the previous one because your train loses energy throughout the ride.

NEAR THE END:
Air resistance, as well as friction between the train and the track, use up some of your train's total energy.

GOING DOWN HILL:
Once your train starts down the hill, gravity takes over. Your train's potential energy now becomes kinetic energy, the energy of motion.

TOTAL LENGTH:
3,118 ft (950 m)
DURATION:
50.6 seconds

U-SHAPED TRACK:
45 stories tall, 90 degrees straight up

CAMEL HUMP:
129 ft (39 m)

SPIRAL:
270 degrees

MAXIMUM ELEVATION:
456 ft (139 m)

More than **3,500 ROLLER COASTERS** thrill riders around the world. Asia has more roller coasters than North America and Europe combined. China has the **MOST COASTERS** overall, but the Netherlands and United Kingdom have the most coasters per person.

WANT TO KNOW MORE?

TELL ME MORE

AIR TIME AND OTHER CRAZINESS

The twists, turns, and loops of a roller coaster mess with you. They keep changing your ride's speed and position to give you butterflies in your stomach or smush you down in your seat. What's going on? It's those crazy forces again. Gravity and acceleration mix to push your body in different directions, sometimes making you feel light as a feather—even weightless—and sometimes as heavy as lead. It's part of what makes roller coasters so exciting (or scary).

FEAR FACTOR

You're cruising along on a coaster, and you barely miss one of the coaster's supports. Then you almost blast through a fire. Maybe you narrowly escape capture by an abominable snowman. Close calls! They were made that way on purpose. Roller-coaster designers know that adding a bit of fear to the physical ups and downs makes a roller coaster even more thrilling. The near misses and tight fits also make you feel like you're zooming along out of control. You're not. It's all part of the plan.

TRY THIS!

Nervous about riding a coaster through a loop-de-loop? No worries. You won't fall out. To prove it to yourself, try this. Put a little water in a plastic bucket, and take it outside. Grab the handle and swing the bucket quickly in a circle like it's going through a roller-coaster loop. Did the water dump on you when it was over your head? If you were swinging the bucket fast enough, it shouldn't have. Did you defy gravity? Nope. It's still pulling the water (and bucket) toward Earth. But the force of acceleration at the very top of the loop is stronger, and it's pulling upwards. Inertia, another force, also pushes the water to the outside of the loop. You stay dry! And the water didn't even have a safety harness.

The fastest roller coaster in the world is the **Formula Rossa,** which clocks in at **149 miles an hour** (240 km/h). It's so intense that riders **must wear goggles** to protect their eyes.

FUN FACTS

The **Cyclone,** which opened at New York's Coney Island in **1927,** is one of the **greatest coasters** ever made. Reaching **60 miles an hour** (97 km/h) and featuring steep drops and lots of "air time," this historic spot still attracts thrill-seekers.

The Cyclone

FORCES IN MOTION

As you zip up and down and around the tracks, forces pull you in all different directions. Find out how the changing forces make for a fun ride.

GOING UPHILL:
You feel really heavy when you're speeding up a steep hill because the force of acceleration, which pushes you back into your seat, and gravity work together to pull you back.

TOP OF HILL:
At the top of a hill, you may get some "air time," lifting out of your seat (as far as the safety restraints allow) for a moment, because your body still wants to climb, even though the train already is heading down.

GOING DOWNHILL:
When you plunge down a steep hill, you feel weightless for a moment as the force of gravity pulling you down balances the force of acceleration, which pushes you up into your seat.

TOP OF LOOP-DE-LOOP:
When you're upside down at the top of a loop, you feel as light as a feather. The reason is that gravity is pulling you out of your seat, toward the ground, but the force of acceleration is pushing you into your seat, toward the clouds.

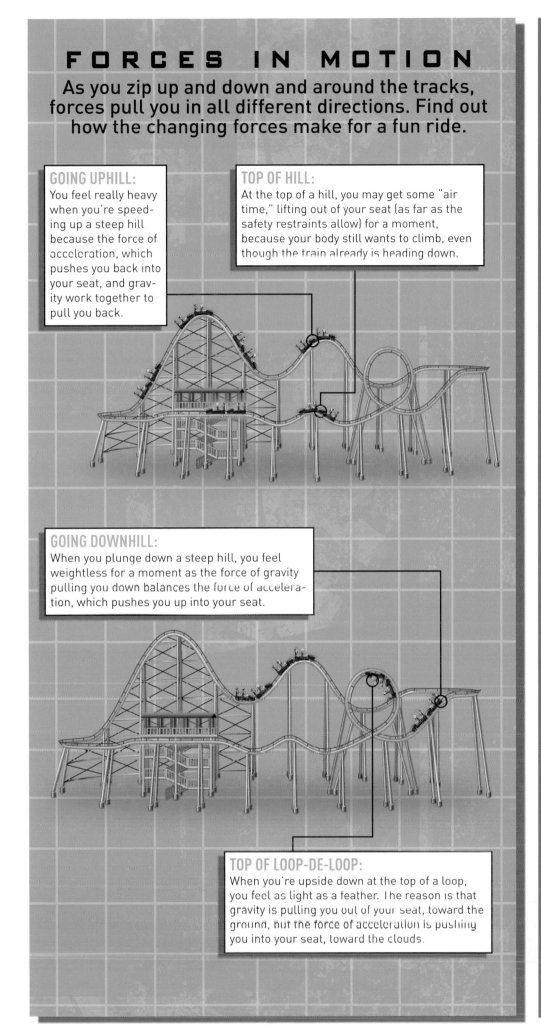

How Things Worked

The inspiration for today's roller coasters was really cool. As far back as the 1400s, Russians sought their thrills on towering slides coated with thick ice. The slides grew to 70 to 80 feet (21 to 24 m) tall and had drops as steep as modern roller coasters. Riders climbed to the top, hopped on a sled made of wood or an ice block covered with straw, and careened down the steep slide at crazy speeds. Russian ruler Catherine the Great loved the thrill and had several built on her property. It was only a matter of time before someone looked for a way to make it a year-round activity. The Switchback, which thrilled riders in St. Petersburg, Russia, in the late 1700s, had carriages that ran in grooved tracks over a hilly course. It didn't take long for these roller coasters to catch on. The French started building roller coasters in the early 1800s. In 1817, they opened two coasters with big innovations. In one, called the Russian Mountains of Belleville, the cars' wheels had extra-long axles that locked into grooves on the inside of the tracks. The other, called the Aerial Walk, featured the first circular track, though ride attendants had to push the cars back to the top. These innovations were such a big deal that Paris is often called the birthplace of the modern roller coaster.

Russian ice slides

TALES FROM THE LAB

UPPING THE THRILL FACTOR:
ROLLER COASTER INNOVATIONS

In 1958, engineers at Disneyland received a postcard from their boss, Walt Disney. On the front was a picture of Switzerland's most famous mountain, the pyramid-shaped Matterhorn. On the back, Walt had written, "Build this!"

Walt didn't just want a mountain. He wanted bobsleds racing down it.

There was just one problem. It wasn't the mountain—Disney engineers could build that. But how could they make the clackety, rumbly wooden roller coasters of the time feel like bobsleds whooshing down iced tracks?

Disney designers turned to Karl Bacon and Ed Morgan, two of the partners in a small machine shop called Arrow Development. Arrow

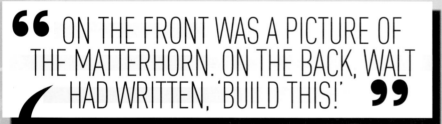

> ON THE FRONT WAS A PICTURE OF THE MATTERHORN. ON THE BACK, WALT HAD WRITTEN, 'BUILD THIS!'

had a reputation for making just about anything, from electronic parts to huge furnaces to Disneyland's first rides. One guy even asked them to grind down his false teeth. (They said no.)

Karl and Ed knew they couldn't make a fast, smooth-running coaster on flat or L-shaped iron rails and wood—the way coaster tracks were made back then. They brainstormed and tested new ideas, and they discovered the solution: hollow steel tubes. Steel tubes could be bent into any shape.

They made the perfect dips and turns for the Matterhorn bobsleds.

The Matterhorn was a hit. And Arrow's tubular track design forever changed thrill rides.

ARROW DEVELOPMENT FINDS A NEW TWIST

With tubular tracks, roller coasters could go faster through tight twists and turns and drops. That got Karl Bacon thinking: Why not make a coaster go upside down?

Looping coasters had been tried before, in the mid-1800s and early 1900s, with disastrous results. Some carried too few passengers to make money. Others were uncomfortable or even dangerous. One train fell off its track on its first trip.

And now Bacon wanted to send passengers through two 360-degree rolls on a corkscrew-shaped track. If they didn't get the shape exactly right, it would never work.

It was the mid-1970s, with no computer programs to help them, so Arrow engineers built a model. They wrapped a rod around a pipe that was 12 inches (30 cm) in diameter to get the shape and then put a small metal car on it. Karl experimented with different angles and calculated the speeds through the corkscrew. He needed enough speed to keep the passengers in their seats but not give them whiplash.

When Karl thought he got it right, Arrow built a full-size corkscrew. It looked good but pretty extreme. They were nervous about riding it. A worker put a tire in the seat—it was the corkscrew's first passenger. The tire swirled through the rolls without flying out, so two engineers climbed aboard. One ride, and they knew they had another hit.

When the owners of Knott's Berry Farm theme park in California, U.S.A., saw the corkscrew, they bought it on the spot. Corkscrews and loops soon popped up at amusement parks around the world.

IN 1912, COASTER ENGINEER **JOHN MILLER** FIGURED OUT HOW TO LOCK COASTER CARS TO THE TRACKS SO THEY COULD GO FASTER AND **TAKE STEEPER DROPS AND SHARPER CURVES.** MILLER'S INNOVATION, THE **"UPSTOP WHEEL,"** LAUNCHED THE "GOLDEN AGE" OF ROLLER COASTERS IN THE 1920s.

ARROW DEVELOPMENT DESIGNED A **LOG FLUME RIDE,** BUT THEY COULDN'T GET PERMISSION TO BUILD A LARGE WATER RESERVOIR TO TEST IT. NO PROBLEM. THEY BUILT A **SMALL MODEL** AND USED WATER FROM A SWIMMING POOL.

THE ORIGINAL **CORKSCREW** ROLLER COASTER—A PRETTY TAME RIDE BY TODAY'S STANDARDS—**STILL THRILLS RIDERS.** IT MOVED FROM KNOTT'S BERRY FARM TO SILVERWOOD THEME PARK IN IDAHO IN 1990.

The Windjammer, Buena Park, California, U.S.A.

Make It BETTER!

Giant drops, loop-de-loops, or dangling feet—everyone's got different tastes when it comes to their favorite coasters. Maybe you like simple wooden coasters that take you over hills and steep drops. Or maybe you prefer something more sophisticated—where you wait in line in a space station and take off to outer space like at Walt Disney World's Space Mountain.

Some engineers make a living designing these awesome rides! They make sure the roller coasters you love are fast, fun, and safe. Now it's your turn. What would your ideal roller coaster look like? Would it be superfast or have lots of turns and loops? Grab a pencil and paper and sketch your idea—you might have what it takes to be the next great roller-coaster designer!

A BOBSLED WITH NOISY WHEELS? NO WAY. THE MATTERHORN'S BUILDERS USED A LAYER OF A NEWLY INVENTED MATERIAL, **POLYURETHANE,** ON THE SLEDS' METAL WHEELS. THAT'S THE SAME STUFF THAT YOUR SKATEBOARD WHEELS ARE MADE OF. ANOTHER MATTERHORN INNOVATION.

HANG TEN

How does SURFING let you conquer the waves?

Check It Out!

What could be cooler than riding through the barrel of a breaker? It's just you and your board, riding down the tube, the wave breaking over your head. Surfing's the ultimate ride. But how in the world do you do it? Find out what goes into catching a wave.

How do surfboards work **?**

Can I surf any wave **?**

How do I stay on the board **?**

Surfing's easy. But surfing while dancing? Now that's a challenge ...

JUST THE FACTS

Riding a Wave

A good surfer makes it look so easy, but there's a lot to riding a wave. You paddle to the wave. If you catch it, you pop up into position, left foot forward if you're "natural-footed" or right foot forward if you're "goofy-footed." If you're not positioned just right, you can't make decent turns or have enough momentum to ride the wave—and that's if you don't wipe out. You need to keep your balance. It helps to spread your arms and to crouch to lower your center of gravity. Your board needs to be able to handle the waves you're chasing, and you need to be able to handle the board. And you definitely have to know your waves. That's what surfing is all about.

Board, Yet?

So, are you going to hit the waves on a thruster, malibu, fish, or gun? Tough choice. They're all awesome surfboards, light and strong with a foam core and a fiberglass coat. But each is designed to handle the waves in a different way. The thruster is a shortboard, usually between five feet eight inches (1.75 m) and six feet ten inches (2 m) long. It's best at quick maneuvers on waves. The malibu, or "mal"—a good choice for beginners—is a thicker longboard with a rounded front. It's more stable, so it's easier to stand on. The fish is similar to a shortboard but shorter and wider. The gun is a big shortboard, ready to handle the biggest waves. Wow! Now that you've picked a board, you just need to decide on the kind of nose, deck, rails, tail, wax, leash ...

A **"SHAPER"** is someone who hand-makes a **SURFBOARD.**

IF IN DOUBT PADDLE OUT

There's a lot more to surfing than just **grabbing a board** and **catching a wave,** and choosing the right surfboard is the first step. Surfboards come in all shapes and sizes, from the easy-to-maneuver shortboard to the versatile longboard (and everything in between). Here's how some of the most popular surfboards measure up!

Good for small waves

Popular with the pros!

Great for beginners!

Fish
LENGTH: 5'2" to 6'4"
(157.5 cm–193.0 cm)
WIDTH: 20" to 22"
(50.8 cm–55.9 cm)

Shortboard
LENGTH: 5' to 6'10"
(152.4 cm–208.3 cm)
WIDTH: 16" to 19"
(40.6 cm–48.3 cm)

Fun board
LENGTH: 6'6" to 8'
(198.1 cm–243.8 cm)
WIDTH: 20" to 22"
(50.8 cm–55.9 cm)

FUN FACT

"HANG TEN" MEANS PUTTING **ALL YOUR TOES** OVER THE NOSE OF A LONGBOARD. YOU CAN ALSO **"HANG FIVE"** IF YOU DO IT WITH ONLY ONE FOOT.

DESIGNED FOR AWESOME

Every part of your board is designed to make your ride totally, totally awesome, dude.

DECK:
The deck is the surface you stand on. It's not flat but is shaped in ways to help the board move. Special wax keeps you from slipping off. Some decks even have soft tops in case you bump on them when you wipe out.

TAIL:
The tail's shape affects how your board moves in the water.

NOSE:
The board's front tip, its nose, can be pointed or rounded and swoop up a little or a lot. The shape affects how the board goes into a wave and how easy it is to paddle.

RAILS:
The outer edges of the board are called rails. Larger rails make it easier for the board to float, while narrow rails sink a little, making it easier to lean.

BOTTOM:
The bottom of the board is shaped to match how you like to catch waves. A slightly cup-shaped bottom, like on a boat, provides a smoother ride. A curve going the opposite way, so that it's higher in the middle, makes the board move faster.

FINS:
Surfboards have one or more fins to keep the board moving forward instead of sliding side-ways. If your board has three fins, you've got a thruster.

LEG ROPE:
A leash attaches the surfboard to your leg, so it doesn't get away when you wipe out.

Easy to paddle, but tough to turn

Longboard
LENGTH: 8' to 9'
(243.8 cm–274.3 cm)

WANT TO KNOW MORE?

TELL ME MORE

ON THE SAME WAVELENGTH

Here's the secret to serious surfing: You want to ride swell, not some rubbish wind chop. Got it? No? Well, then, let's take a closer look at waves—oh, and learn a little surfer slang along the way. Wind creates waves. If the wind is way out in the ocean, far offshore, the waves it makes will travel many miles across the open ocean before reaching you and your surfboard. As they travel, they become more organized, widely spaced, and cleaner. These waves are swell. (Really. It's short for groundswell.) They are the perfect waves for surfing. If, on the other hand, the wind is blowing toward the beach, onshore, it creates wind swell. These waves are a mess. They're not organized, they're not shaped well, and they're hard to surf. They are, as surfers say, rubbish wind chop.

BREAKING POINT

As swell, or groundswell, rolls toward the beach, the waves in front get dragged along the sea-floor and slow down. The waves following them start to ride up their backs, getting taller and taller. As a wave builds, it eventually gets too steep to support itself, and it starts to spill forward. That's a breaker. If you can get your board on the face of that wave, right before the break, you've got a chance at catching a tube ride. Awesome, dude.

TRY THIS!

It's easy to see how wind creates waves. Fill a sink with a couple of inches (about 5 cm or so) of water and blow across it to make waves. If you blow several puffs, you may even create a stream of waves—just like in the ocean.

FUN FACTS

● Early travelers' descriptions of Hawaiian surfing as **"the most supreme pleasure"** may have inspired **Thomas Jefferson** to include "the pursuit of happiness" as an inalienable right in the **U.S. Declaration of Independence.**

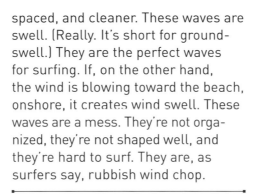

Thomas Jefferson

● The famous American humorist **Mark Twain** wrote in 1866 that he had tried surfing **"but made a failure of it."**

Mark Twain

● Surfing became a **craze** in the United States in the **1960s.** Surfing and California beach culture became popularized in "beach movies" and in "surf music" by groups like **The Beach Boys.**

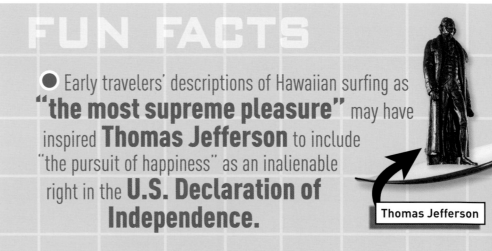

The Beach Boys

TAKING A BREAKER

The best surf waves are swells that start way far out in the ocean.

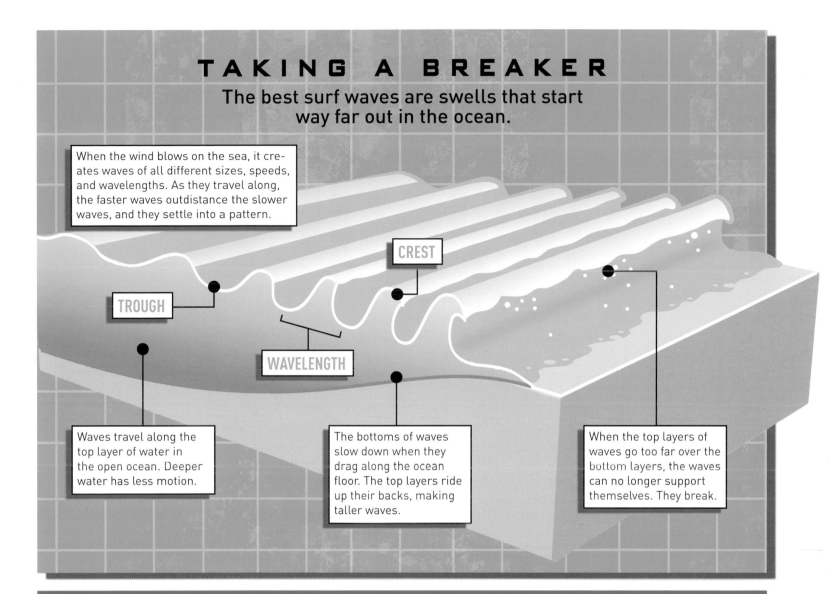

When the wind blows on the sea, it creates waves of all different sizes, speeds, and wavelengths. As they travel along, the faster waves outdistance the slower waves, and they settle into a pattern.

CREST

TROUGH

WAVELENGTH

Waves travel along the top layer of water in the open ocean. Deeper water has less motion.

The bottoms of waves slow down when they drag along the ocean floor. The top layers ride up their backs, making taller waves.

When the top layers of waves go too far over the bottom layers, the waves can no longer support themselves. They break.

How Things Worked

People were riding the waves long before anyone thought to say, "Surf's up, dude!" More than 3,000 years ago, fishermen in western Polynesia rode wooden boards to shore with their catch. When Polynesians migrated to Hawaii thirteen centuries later, they brought their boards with them. Hawaiians loved "wave sliding." Over the next few centuries, surfing became more than a pastime. Hawaiian chiefs used it to show their strength and their command over their people. They rode long surfboards crafted from light and buoyant wood, while commoners got smaller boards made of heavier and denser wood. Although an important part of Hawaiian culture, surfing almost died out. European explorers started arriving in the 1770s, bringing diseases that wiped out much of the Hawaiian population. Surfing nearly vanished by the late 1800s. Then, in 1905, Duke Kahanamoku, who later became an Olympic swimming champion and world-record holder, helped revive surfing in Hawaii as one of the famous "Beach Boys of Waikiki." Duke rode a traditional Hawaiian board more than twice his height. A couple of years later, Irish Hawaiian George Freeth introduced surfing to California. He cut a traditional 16-foot (4.9-m) board in half, sparking a revolution in surfboard design and surfing techniques. Soon afterward, board shapers started experimenting. They made boards in all different sizes, shapes, and materials— perfect for anyone daring enough to tackle the waves.

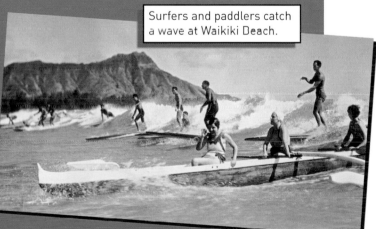

Surfers and paddlers catch a wave at Waikiki Beach.

FAKESTER

How does a SIMULATOR feel so real?

Check It Out!

Where can you blast off into space, go back to the time of dinosaurs, soar above the mountains, explore inside a human body, or hang out with your favorite superhero? You guessed it: a simulator ride. A simulator is a thrill ride that stays in one place, but it feels like a real adventure. Fasten your seat belt! It's time to find out how a simulator can take you on a rollicking ride—without even leaving the ground.

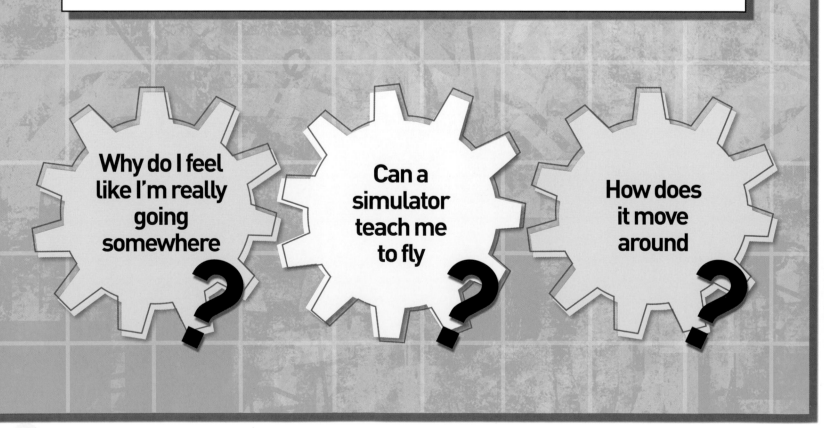

Why do I feel like I'm really going somewhere ?

Can a simulator teach me to fly ?

How does it move around ?

JUST THE FACTS

Adventure Maker

It's your turn to ride. You enter the capsule, settle into a seat, and strap on your safety harness. The door clicks shut, and the lights dim. The capsule powers up. Your heart starts to beat a little faster, and you take off. You climb and plunge. You zoom past obstacles. Your body sways with the motion of the capsule. You watch the view in front of you. You're on an amazing adventure, and it's all thanks to the simulator. The simulator is programmed to move you—either your seat or the entire capsule—to match the action on the screen. The motion, sights, and sounds (and maybe even smells and other special effects!) trick your mind into thinking you're really riding a roller coaster, soaring through space, or traveling back in time.

Who's in Charge?

Some simulators, like a racing car game, have controls you use to tell the vehicle how to move. A computer reads your commands and moves the simulator to match your directions. This type is called an interactive simulator. Other simulators, like those at museums and amusement parks, plunge you into a story or make you feel as if you're riding a roller coaster or soaring on a hang glider. A computer program, which an attendant runs, tells the simulator what to do. This type is called a passive simulator. Both kinds pack in lots of thrills.

Not Just Fun and Games

Simulators may be a lot of fun, but they also can be serious work. Simulators originally were made to train people to do difficult things, and they're still used for that. Many pilots train on flight simulators before they take to the skies in a real jet. Astronauts also practice things that are hard to do, like fixing a satellite, in a simulated environment. Even teenagers learning to drive may take a spin in a simulator before they hit the road in a real car. Simulators provide a safe way to learn skills to use on the road, in the sky, or up in space.

FUN FACT
NASA'S **AMES RESEARCH CENTER,** IN CALIFORNIA, U.S.A., HAS AN ADVANCED SIMULATOR THAT CAN REPRODUCE THE ACTIONS OF ANY KIND OF **FLYING CRAFT,** WHETHER IT'S A FIGHTER JET, HELICOPTER, SPACE SHUTTLE, OR BLIMP. THE SIMULATOR MOVES 60 FEET (18 M) UP AND DOWN AND 40 FEET (12 M) SIDE TO SIDE.

MAKING YOU BELIEVE

A simulator ride feels like a real adventure. See how a computer program and actual movement work together to trick your brain.

SPEAKERS: Speakers supply the sound effects for your adventure.

SEAT/SAFETY HARNESS: You need to be strapped securely in your seat. Even if the simulator is not really traveling somewhere, it takes you on a rollicking ride.

SCREEN: Realistic images let you watch your adventure play out. The images usually are made by an artist using a computer, so it can easily mimic the adventure.

BASE/MOTION PLATFORM: A platform, controlled by the computer, moves the capsule to match what you see and hear.

TRUCK DRIVER training schools are starting to follow suit. In fact, when Schneider National introduced simulator training for its truck drivers, it saw a **21% DECREASE** in preventable accidents on the road!

WORK HARD PLAY HARD

Some professionals use simulators to help them train. For airline pilots, flight simulators can be useful supplements to actual flights. For astronauts, simulations are essential for knowing what to do in outer space. (It's not like they can **take a test flight to space!**)

Average time using simulation:

ASTRONAUT: 300 hours

AIRLINE PILOT: 50–100 hours

WANT TO KNOW MORE?

TELL ME MORE

GETTING REAL

Motion simulators are a type of "virtual reality," or "VR." In computer talk, something that is virtual doesn't exist physically. It's made to seem that way by computer programs using advanced technology. VR taps into our senses to fool our brains. We feel like we're in the virtual world, moving around and experiencing it. We can see it, hear it, and sometimes even smell it. We maybe even can touch things and move them around. But a simulator ride is not the only way to experience virtual reality. Companies are making VR headsets to use with games or to let us watch sports as if we were right there on the sidelines.

A MOVING EXPERIENCE

A computer may tell the simulator how to move, but it's usually hydraulics that does the heavy lifting. Hydraulics uses a liquid, usually a type of oil, to move things. Why a liquid? It's kind of a Goldilocks thing. Gases squish too easily. Solids are way too hard. But liquids are just right. They move easily from place to place, but they don't squish. In scientific terms, they're "incompressible"; they can't be pressed into something smaller. When a liquid is trapped inside of something like a cylinder, it can do a lot of work. If you push a liquid down the cylinder, it can push something on the other end. Where hydraulics gets really interesting—and really useful—is when you change the shape of the container. The liquid's pressure doesn't change inside the container, no matter how it's shaped. So you can push the liquid through a long, narrow tube into a larger cylinder, and it will be able to move something much bigger at the other end. Its force gets multiplied.

TRY THIS!

Flight simulators don't just train pilots how to zoom through the sky. They also train the pilots how to navigate using an airplane's instruments—and that's really important. Pilots can't always trust their sight alone. If they stare at one spot, like a light or star, when it's totally dark around it, their sense of sight can be tricked into thinking the light is moving—an autokinetic illusion, a type of optical illusion that makes something look like it's moving. You can simulate an experience like this for yourself. Stare at this picture to see how easy it is to trick your sense of sight.

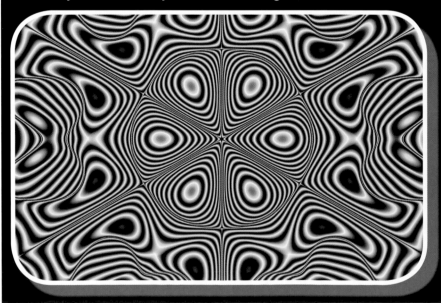

FUN FACTS

● **Early flight simulators,** made in the 1930s and 1940s by Edwin Link, were nicknamed the **"blue box"** for their bright blue paint. Some also had yellow wings.

● When you see a word that starts with *hydro* or *hydr*, it's something to do **with liquid.** It's from the Greek word for **"water."**

HYDROPOWER

Liquid under pressure can apply a lot of force—enough to move a simulator. That's why most motion simulators use a hydraulic system to create their motion. Check out how it works.

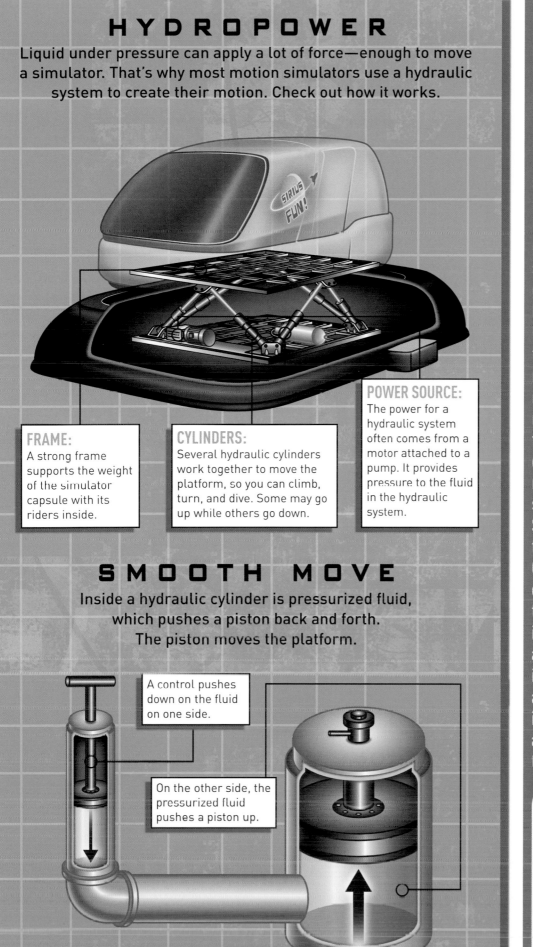

FRAME:
A strong frame supports the weight of the simulator capsule with its riders inside.

CYLINDERS:
Several hydraulic cylinders work together to move the platform, so you can climb, turn, and dive. Some may go up while others go down.

POWER SOURCE:
The power for a hydraulic system often comes from a motor attached to a pump. It provides pressure to the fluid in the hydraulic system.

SMOOTH MOVE

Inside a hydraulic cylinder is pressurized fluid, which pushes a piston back and forth.
The piston moves the platform.

A control pushes down on the fluid on one side.

On the other side, the pressurized fluid pushes a piston up.

Viddy-up horsey!

PROFILE: Edwin Link

No one could fly in weather like that: The sky was thick with dark clouds, and a winter's rain beat down.

A group of U.S. Army Air Corps officials, waiting for a demonstration of a flight trainer, turned to leave. They figured the pilot had given up and gone back. In 1934, pilots needed to see where they were going. Nasty weather made that impossible.

> **"ED TRAINED TO FLY IN THE FIRST-EVER FLIGHT SIMULATOR, ONE HE HAD MADE WITH HIS OWN HANDS."**

But then they heard it: the hum of an aircraft engine. A plane emerged from the clouds and came in for a smooth landing. The pilot, Ed Link, was waving.

Ed had just proved that, if properly trained, pilots could "fly blind," using airplane instruments to guide their flight when they couldn't see the ground. They could fly in bad weather, like he had done for 200 miles (322 km).

Ed had trained to fly by using instruments in a flight simulator—the first-ever, and one he had made with his own hands with parts from a pipe organ.

It was a success. The Air Corps put in an order for Link Trainers. It was the break Ed had been waiting for.

SETTING HIS MIND

Ed was born in 1904, seven months after the Wright brothers took their historic first flight. As a boy, he spent hours experimenting, figuring out how gadgets worked, and exploring.

The dreamer didn't fit in at his school, where they wanted kids to memorize fact after fact. Facts were already known! Ed wanted to explore the unknown. He especially wanted to fly.

But that was the last thing his father wanted. Ed and his older brother were supposed to get the finest educations available and learn all about business, so they could take over the family's piano and organ factory.

Ed refused. He was happy to go to a vocational school, where he could learn engineering skills and create things with his own hands. But he refused to stay at the stuffy schools his dad preferred. When he was a teen, his mother took him to California to enroll him in the Los Angeles Polytechnic Institute, a vocational training school.

Later, he went to work at his dad's factory, but not in the business office. He built organs and tuned pianos. Soon he was designing new organs for theaters. He got a patent for a device that cleaned player piano rolls. But he still wanted to fly.

IDEAS THAT SOARED

When he was 16, he spent all his earnings on one flying lesson. The pilot put Ed in the second seat of his little biplane and roared into the sky. The plane did loops and spins and zoomed low over buildings. Ed was scared to death but fascinated. After they landed, Ed realized he had never even touched the controls. Some lesson!

While he worked on organs, he kept thinking about that first lesson. "Would-be pilots for the most part simply climbed into airplanes and tried to learn by the seat of their pants," Ed's biographer wrote. Some student pilots didn't survive their in-air training.

Ed managed to learn to fly, but he knew there had to be a better way. After working all day at the organ factory, he'd go into its basement and work late into the night designing and building a flight trainer. He made it bank and turn using the things he knew best: parts from pipe organs. After 18 months, he had created the first realistic flight simulator.

It was impressive. The famous pilot Casey Jones bought six. But hardly anyone else did. Ed started taking it to county fairs and charging a quarter per ride.

Casey called up some officials he knew in the Air Corps. He convinced them to come to the airstrip on that rainy winter's day in 1934 to see a flight demonstration. The rest was up to Ed. Ed soared into the rain and made history.

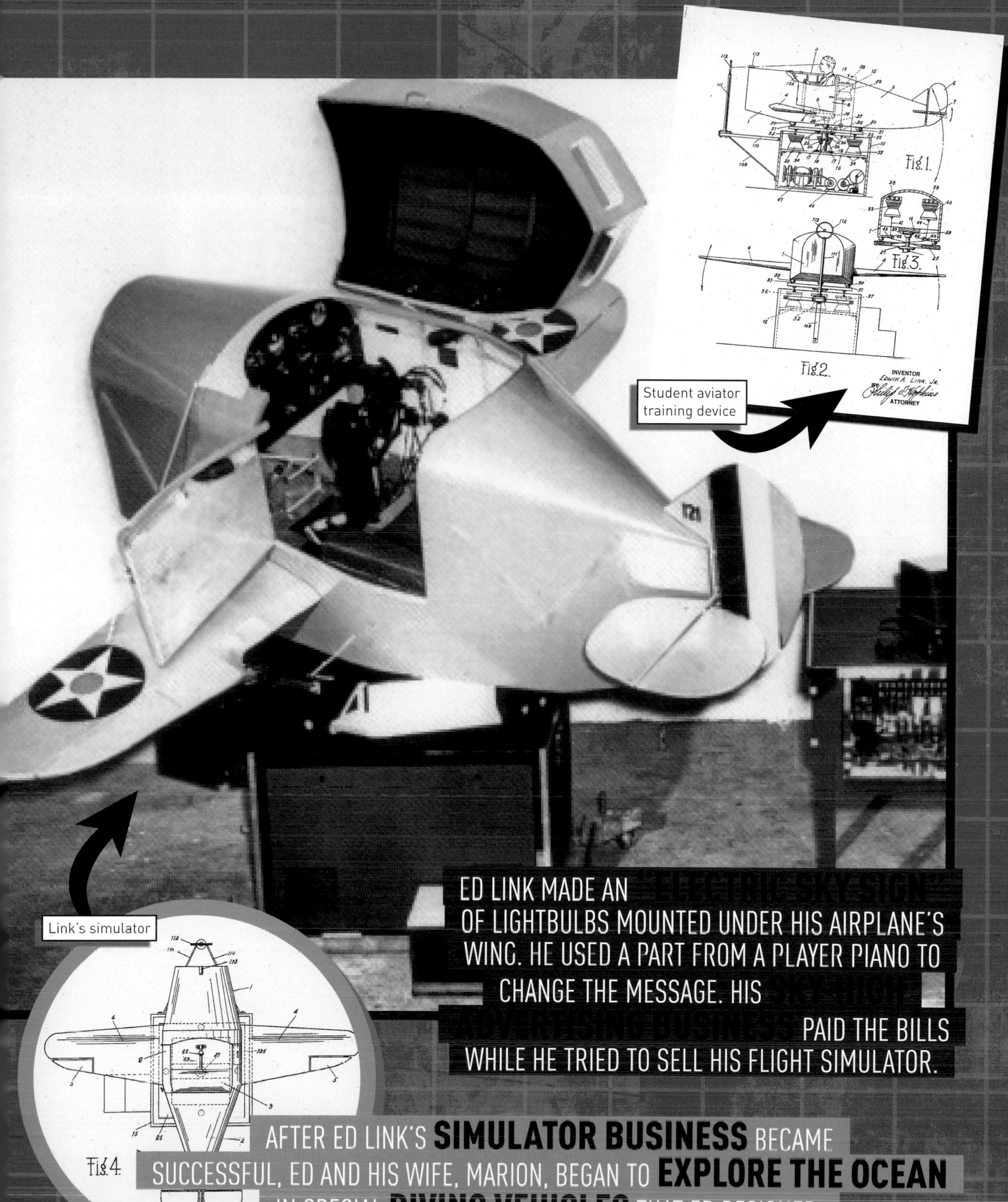

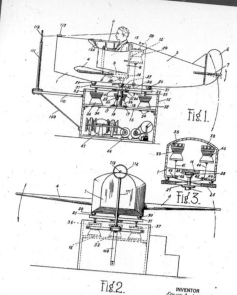

Student aviator training device

Fig.1.

Fig.2.

Fig.3.

INVENTOR
EDWIN A. LINK, JR.

ATTORNEY

Link's simulator

Fig.4.

ED LINK MADE AN ELECTRIC SKY SIGN OF LIGHTBULBS MOUNTED UNDER HIS AIRPLANE'S WING. HE USED A PART FROM A PLAYER PIANO TO CHANGE THE MESSAGE. HIS SKY-HIGH ADVERTISING BUSINESS PAID THE BILLS WHILE HE TRIED TO SELL HIS FLIGHT SIMULATOR.

AFTER ED LINK'S **SIMULATOR BUSINESS** BECAME SUCCESSFUL, ED AND HIS WIFE, MARION, BEGAN TO **EXPLORE THE OCEAN** IN SPECIAL **DIVING VEHICLES** THAT ED DESIGNED.

JUMPING FOR JOY

How do BOUNCE HOUSES boost us so high?

Check It Out!

Bounce around on a big balloon? It sounds crazy—and like a lot of fun. That's the idea behind bounce houses, those inflated playgrounds where you can jump and flip on a cushion of air. Do you know how they get the bounce in the house? Read on before you jump to conclusions.

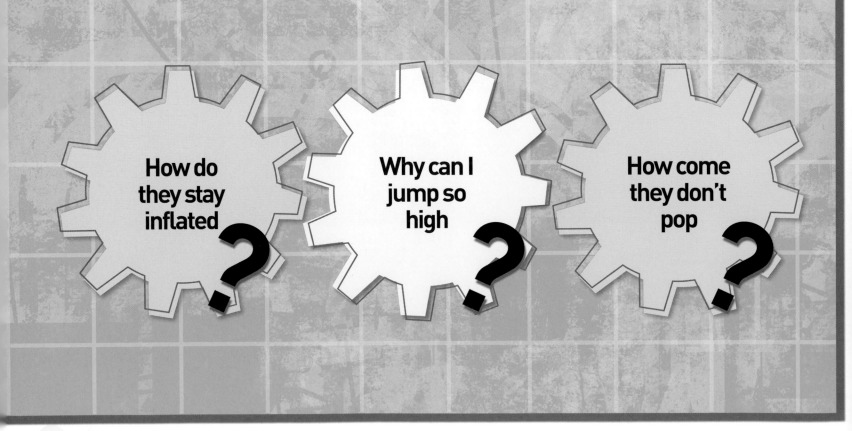

How do they stay inflated?

Why can I jump so high?

How come they don't pop?

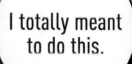

JUST THE FACTS

Fun by Leaps and Bounds

How do you create a balloon so big that people can climb on top? Luckily, you don't have to blow one up with your mouth like a regular balloon! You use a special air blower powered by electricity. The blower works the entire time you're jumping to make sure the house stays properly inflated. Inflated columns and mesh walls make sure your jumps don't carry you away.

Can It Pop?

Uh-oh. Do you hear hissing? No need to worry. The bounce house is not about to pop. Bounce houses are made to take a lot of punishment. Their surfaces are made of thick, strong materials like vinyl and nylon. And they're designed to leak! A little bit of air escapes through the seams all the time, so you have to keep the air blower on the whole time you're jumping. Not only can they handle all those people jumping around, but even small punctures aren't a problem.

A European company makes a 16-foot (5-m)-wide **INFLATABLE CHURCH** complete with a 40-foot (12-m)-tall steeple. No, it's **NOT FOR JUMPING**. It's to let people get married "wherever their hearts desire."

What DO YOU call it?

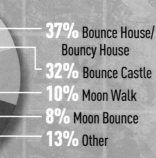

- **37%** Bounce House/ Bouncy House
- **32%** Bounce Castle
- **10%** Moon Walk
- **8%** Moon Bounce
- **13%** Other

AN INFLATABLE BY ANY OTHER NAME ...

Bouncy House. Moon Bounce. Bounce Castle. It goes by many names. That's why we polled people on the streets of Washington, D.C., to find out which names are the most popular!

FUN FACT

THE UNITED KINGDOM AND AUSTRALIA REQUIRE BOUNCE HOUSES TO HAVE **WALLS ON THREE SIDES** BUT AN OPEN FRONT WITH FOAM **"CRASH MATS"** TO CATCH KIDS WHO JUMP OR FALL OUT.

GETTING A LIFT

A bounce house gets its bounciness because it's filled with air, like a big balloon.

BOUNCE HOUSE:
Inflated columns and netting help keep you safe while you jump.

SEAMS:
A little air escapes out of the seams, making a small hissing sound.

AIR BLOWER:
An air blower pumps air into the bounce house the entire time you're jumping.

FUN FACT

FRENCH ARCHITECTS DESIGNED AN **INFLATABLE TRAMPOLINE BRIDGE** BIG ENOUGH TO SPAN PARIS'S FAMOUS SEINE RIVER. THE CONCEPT IS BEING TESTED IN SPAIN, BUT THE REAL BRIDGE HASN'T BEEN BUILT—AND THERE'S NO GUARANTEE IT WILL BE.

WANT TO KNOW MORE?

TELL ME MORE

BOUNDLESS ENERGY

Why do you bounce so high in the bounce house? It's all about energy. When you're in a bounce house, you actually have more potential energy—the stored-up energy that's kind of like fuel in your tank—than when you're on flat ground. That extra boost of potential energy comes from the springiness of the bounce house. It's like you and the bounce house are a team working together to get you into the air. As the springy surface pushes you up, it transfers its energy to you, and you jump extra high. The potential energy (yours and the bounce house's combined) gets converted to kinetic energy, the energy of motion, as you push off the floor. It's what you use to make those amazing jumps.

TRY THIS!

A simple balloon lets you see bounce power in action. Blow up a balloon and tie it. Hold it between your hands with only one finger on each side of the balloon. Hold tight and squish it down. Quickly pull your fingers away. Did the balloon bounce up? When you squished it down, you increased the balloon's potential energy. When you no longer held it, all that energy converted to kinetic energy, and up the balloon went!

Jumping on an Opportunity

In 1959, mechanical engineer John Scurlock noticed some of his employees goofing off. He didn't get mad. He got inspired. John had been working on a tennis court cover that could be packed up tight but whipped out at the first hint of rain. He made it inflatable. But the big cushion was too tempting for his fun-loving employees to resist. They loved jumping on it. John and his wife, Frances, quickly rented a warehouse and started making "Moonwalks" to rent out. At first, the Moonwalks were just big, inflatable mattresses, but in the late 1960s, they added walls. The company went on to make lots of different inflatable products. John was most proud of the safety air cushion used by fire and rescue departments to catch people who have to jump from buildings.

A firefighter jumps onto an air rescue cushion from the fourth floor of a building during training.

SERIOUS FUN

When you're jumping up and down in a bounce house, you're not just having fun. You're also changing potential energy into kinetic energy and back again.

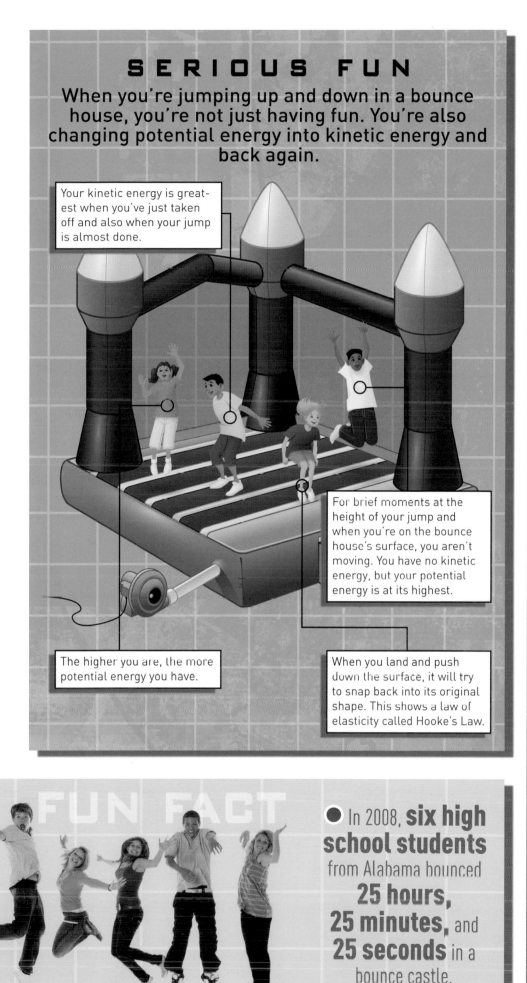

Your kinetic energy is greatest when you've just taken off and also when your jump is almost done.

For brief moments at the height of your jump and when you're on the bounce house's surface, you aren't moving. You have no kinetic energy, but your potential energy is at its highest.

The higher you are, the more potential energy you have.

When you land and push down the surface, it will try to snap back into its original shape. This shows a law of elasticity called Hooke's Law.

FUN FACT

In 2008, **six high school students** from Alabama bounced **25 hours, 25 minutes,** and **25 seconds** in a bounce castle.

Whoa ... SLOW DOWN! A Closer Look at Elasticity

Stretchiness is special. Why, you ask? It's because that ability, called elasticity, involves a lot of energy. Here's how it works: It takes work to push, smush, or pull something out of its original shape. When you do that, you're putting your energy into it and increasing the thing's potential energy, its readiness to do something, like snap back into shape. The moment you step into a bounce house, your weight pushes the floor down. It wants to bounce back up. The same thing happens with the springs on a trampoline. When your weight forces the coils to stretch out, they get more energy. They can use that energy to do their own work. This doesn't only work with things you can jump on. If you pull the string on a bow, you give it the energy to shoot an arrow toward its target. If you dribble a ball, you give it the energy to bounce back up. You put energy in, and the stretchy thing puts it to work—often in a lot of fun ways.

Pushing down on the surface makes it want to push back.

DON'T LOOK DOWN

How does TIGHTROPE WALKING defy gravity?

Check It Out!

Imagine yourself six stories up, a strong metal wire between you and the ground. You take a step and wobble a bit. You hear the gasp of hundreds of spectators below. You take a deep breath. Then another step. You smile and start your tricks. How can anyone do that? Prepare to raise your smarts about tightrope walking.

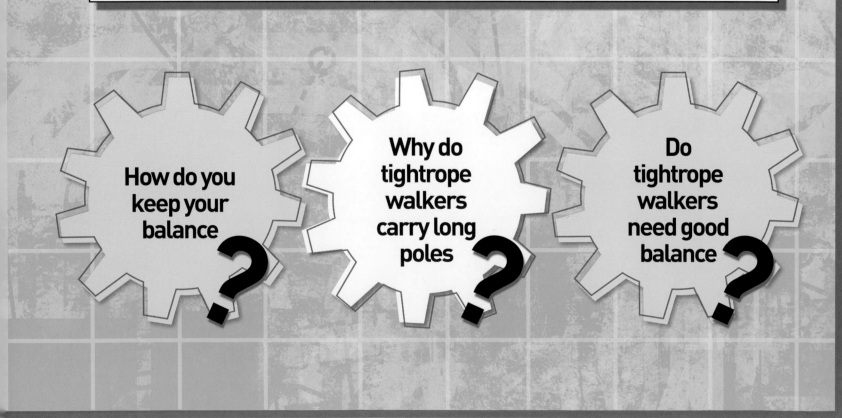

How do you keep your balance ?

Why do tightrope walkers carry long poles ?

Do tightrope walkers need good balance ?

JUST THE FACTS

Balancing Act

It's all about balancing. Think of the wire as something you can rotate, or spin, around. It would be very bad for your health if you did that, so you need to keep centered exactly, precisely, directly above the wire. If you start to wobble, you need to get back into position fast. You can get more time to do that by making it harder for you to spin around the wire. Here's how: Get more mass (it's harder to push over something heavy), and keep it as far from the tightrope as possible (it slows your spin). In other words, carry a balancing stick as long as a school bus and as heavy as your little sister. It'll also lower your center of gravity, or balance point. The droopier, the better.

Starting in the 1850s, Jean François Gravelet, **"THE GREAT BLONDIN,"** crossed Niagara Falls hundreds of times, doing crazier stunts each time. Once he cooked and ate an omelet, complete with stove and neatly set table, on the middle of the wire.

TRY THIS!

First, only try tightrope walking a few inches off the ground. Find a skinny thing to walk on. (Check your nearby play-ground.) Walk along the skinny thing on your own. Try it again hold-ing a pole (a broom's OK) to lower your center of mass. Easier?

HOW'S THE WEATHER UP THERE?

Check out these daring tightrope walkers who **soared above** the rest—literally.

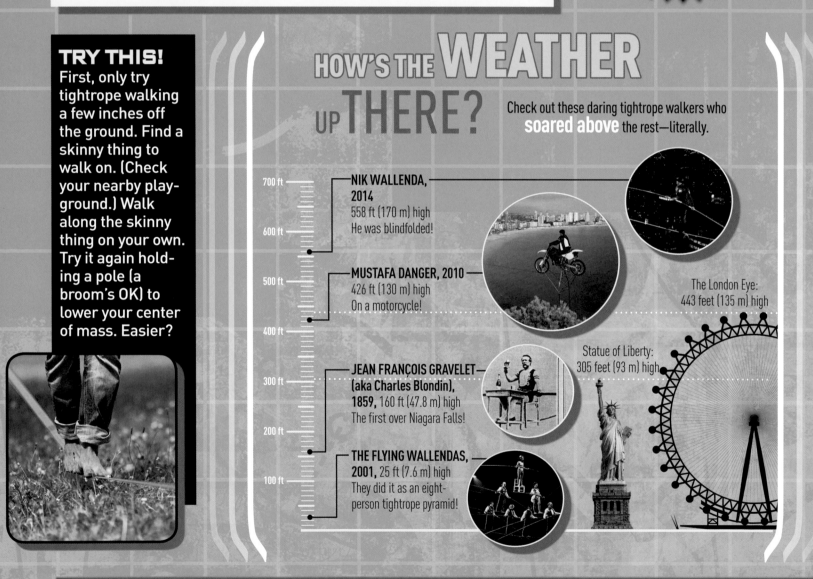

NIK WALLENDA, 2014
558 ft (170 m) high
He was blindfolded!

MUSTAFA DANGER, 2010
426 ft (130 m) high
On a motorcycle!

JEAN FRANCOIS GRAVELET (aka Charles Blondin), 1859, 160 ft (47.8 m) high
The first over Niagara Falls!

THE FLYING WALLENDAS, 2001, 25 ft (7.6 m) high
They did it as an eight-person tightrope pyramid!

The London Eye: 443 feet (135 m) high

Statue of Liberty: 305 feet (93 m) high

700 ft
600 ft
500 ft
400 ft
300 ft
200 ft
100 ft

FUN FACT

THE **TECHNICAL TERM** FOR TIGHTROPE WALKING IS **FUNAMBULISM.** IT'S FROM THE LATIN *FUNIS* (ROPE) AND *AMBULARE* (WALK). SOUNDS FUN, RIGHT?

Let's get all scientific about it. Your mass is the amount of stuff you're made of. Your center of mass is a point that *acts* like all your mass is centered there (even though your mass really is spread throughout your body). You've got to keep your center of mass directly over the wire. When you carry a pole, it's part of your team. It adds to your mass, and it also spreads it out farther from the wire. By adding and spreading, the pole increases your rotational inertia, the force it takes to spin you around the wire. The pole also lowers your center of gravity, your balance point. The more the pole droops, the more it lowers your center of gravity. Some tightrope artists have carried poles so droopy and heavy that their center of gravity is below the wire. They don't even have to worry about balancing!

DEFYING GRAVITY

It may look like a combination of courage and a bit of luck, but tightrope walking also requires a mastery of physics.

A long, droopy pole helps you keep your balance. It lowers your center of gravity and increases your rotational inertia.

Thin, flexible shoes let you curve your feet around the wire while still protecting them from scrapes and bruises.

Some tightropes really are rope, but braided steel cable about a half inch (1.3 cm) thick is more common, especially for long spans.

FUN FACT

One of the **most famous** funambulists of the late 1700s was **Madame Saqui,** who entertained French emperor Napoleon Bonaparte by walking a wire with **fireworks exploding** all around her.

TRY THIS!

MARBLE MADNESS:

DESIGN A LOOPING ROLLER COASTER

Making roller coasters thrilling takes more than imagination. Coasters are amazing works of engineering and science. Every hill, plunge, loop, and curve must be the right size so the train has enough energy to get around the track. You'll get a chance here to find out what's involved. You'll experiment with different designs of coaster loops to see what works best. Ready for a thrill?

WHAT YOU NEED

TIME: about an hour or two

Ask an adult to help.

1. 1.5-inch (3.8-cm) foam pipe insulation, at least 6 feet (2 m) long

2. Duct tape

3. Utility knife

4. Something tall (like a bookcase, chair, stepladder, etc.)

5. Marble

6. Tape measure

7. Pencil and paper

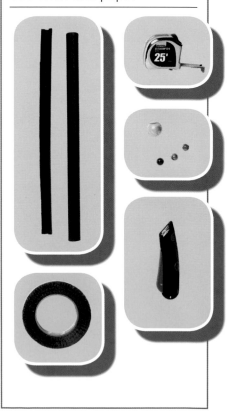

1. HAVE A GROWN-UP CUT the foam pipe insulation in half the long way.

2. TAPE THE FOAM PIPE pieces together end to end to make your track (any length). Make the connections as smooth as possible.

3. SECURE THE BEGINNING OF the track to something tall. (If you want to tape it onto furniture, get a parent's permission!)

4. CURL THE TRACK INTO a loop. Tape the loop together.

5. MEASURE THE HEIGHT OF your loop and how far down the track it is. Write those numbers down.

6. LAUNCH YOUR MARBLE AND see if it can get through the loop. Try it ten times and write down the number of successes.

7. EXPERIMENT! CHANGE THE HEIGHT of the beginning of the track, and do another ten marble runs. Write down how many times the marble made it. See how low you can make the track and still get the marble through the loop.

8. EXPERIMENT SOME MORE! CHANGE the location of the loop in the track or the size of the loop. Keep track of how many times the marble makes it. Tip: Change only one thing at a time. If you change the loop's location, keep the loop the same size.

9. WHAT WORKS BEST? Think about what other cool things you can make your roller coaster do. Give them a try!

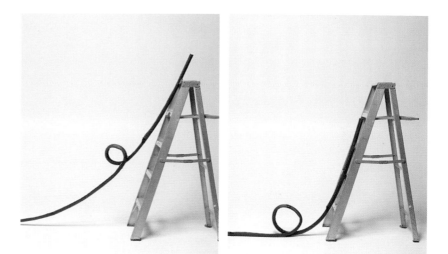

ROLLER COASTERS ARE CONSTANTLY CONVERTING POTENTIAL ENERGY (ENERGY THAT'S STORED UP, KIND OF LIKE FUEL) TO KINETIC ENERGY (ENERGY IN MOTION). WHEN YOUR MARBLE IS AT THE START OF YOUR TRACK, IT HAS A LOT OF POTENTIAL ENERGY. IT'LL NEED KINETIC ENERGY TO GET IT UP AND OVER THE LOOP. DID YOU GIVE IT ENOUGH POTENTIAL ENERGY TO DO THE JOB?

DISNEY'S RIDE DESIGNERS ARE CALLED
"IMAGINEERS": IMAGINATION + ENGINEERS. GET IT?

CHAPTER 5
HERE TO THERE

WE'RE WIRED TO MOVE.
From our earliest days,

we strive to get up on our feet and go.
We want to explore, to seek out new places.
We want to push the limits. How fast can we go?
How far can we go? Is there a better way to get there?
Our history is filled with inventions and innovations
to transport us from here to there. Yesterday's
steam engines gave way to the powerful diesels of today.
And tomorrow? Will we speed along by magnetic
levitation? The sky's the limit. Actually, it's not.
Just hop on a rocket and head on up.

PEDAL POWER

How do BICYCLES transport us?

Check It Out!

Bikes may be the perfect people mover. They can go where cars can't, like up mountain trails or around traffic jams in big cities. They're good for our health (and the Earth's, too). And a whole lot of superbly engineered mobile fun. Bikes have evolved to let us zip along at up to 30 miles an hour (48 km/h), climb mountains, and perform amazing tricks. How do bikes do all this? Prepare to uncover the mysteries of pedal power.

How do a bicycle's gears change its speed ?

Why is it so hard to go uphill ?

Why is it easier to bike right after the tires are pumped up ?

Bike Basics

A bike may not be the fastest thing on the road, but in terms of energy, it's the best. It's not just because it doesn't pollute. A bike is superbly engineered to convert people power into speed. It's an amazing machine. Really. A bike is a "compound machine." It's made of two or more simple machines, those basic devices that apply forces and make them bigger. Bikes do all that—in a very fun way. Pedals, gears, and wheels magnify the force you put into cycling. Handlebars work like a lever to help you turn. The frame distributes your weight so you're balanced. Even the shirt on your back, if it's one of those tight cycling jerseys, helps to allow your bike to move as fast and easily as possible.

BLAST FROM THE PAST. A cycling craze swept America in the late 1880s. But it wasn't socially acceptable for women to straddle the big-wheel, or "penny-farthing," bikes that men rode. Luckily for the ladies, the invention of the "safety bicycle," shaped closer to what we ride now, and special women's bicycling suits put everyone on an equal basis—at least in terms of cycling.

PEDAL PARADISE

Biking isn't just an activity in some parts of the world; it's a **way of life.** Sounds like your kind of place? Maybe you should take a trip to **Denmark** or the **Netherlands.** They're some of the most bike-friendly places around, according to the 2015 Copenhagenize Index, which is based on measurements of safety, bike lanes, and **good feelings.**

Most Bike-Friendly Cities in the World

63% of all members of the Danish Parliament ride their bikes to work in Copenhagen.

The city has 12,000 bike parking spaces (and counting).

Strasbourg Festival of the Bike (Fête du Vélo) takes place every September.

COPENHAGEN, DENMARK

AMSTERDAM, THE NETHERLANDS

UTRECHT, THE NETHERLANDS

STRASBOURG, FRANCE

EINDHOVEN, THE NETHERLANDS

FUN FACT

IN 2013, DUTCH CYCLIST **SEBASTIAAN BOWIER** SET A WORLD-RECORD CYCLING SPEED OF **83.13** MILES AN HOUR (133.78 KM/H). HE RODE THE VELOX 3 RECUMBENT BIKE, THE TYPE YOU LEAN BACK ON, SURROUNDED BY A SHELL THAT REDUCES AIR RESISTANCE.

SCIENCE IN ACTION

All the parts of your bike work together to make it fast and efficient. Check out what goes into pedal power.

HANDLEBARS:
Handlebars work like levers, making it easier to turn your front wheel.

FRAME:
The frame's triangular shape splits your weight between the front and back wheels, so you don't fly over the handlebars when you stop or tip over backwards when you go up a hill. The frame also flexes a little to absorb bumps.

BRAKES:
Brakes stop you by clamping tightly on the wheel's rim when you squeeze the handbrake lever. When the brakes rub against the wheel's rim, they create friction.

PEDALS:
Pedal cranks increase the force from your pedaling.

CHAIN:
The chain transfers the energy from pedaling to the rear wheel, which drives the bike forward

GEARS:
Gears, controlled by a shifter, usually on the handlebars, change the speed or pedaling force.

SPOKES:
Spokes even out the weight on wheels.

TIRES:
Air-filled tires, called pneumatic tires, provide some cushion from bumps.

WHEELS:
The wheel's size multiplies the force of pedaling. The larger the wheel, the more ground the bike covers with each turn of the pedal crank.

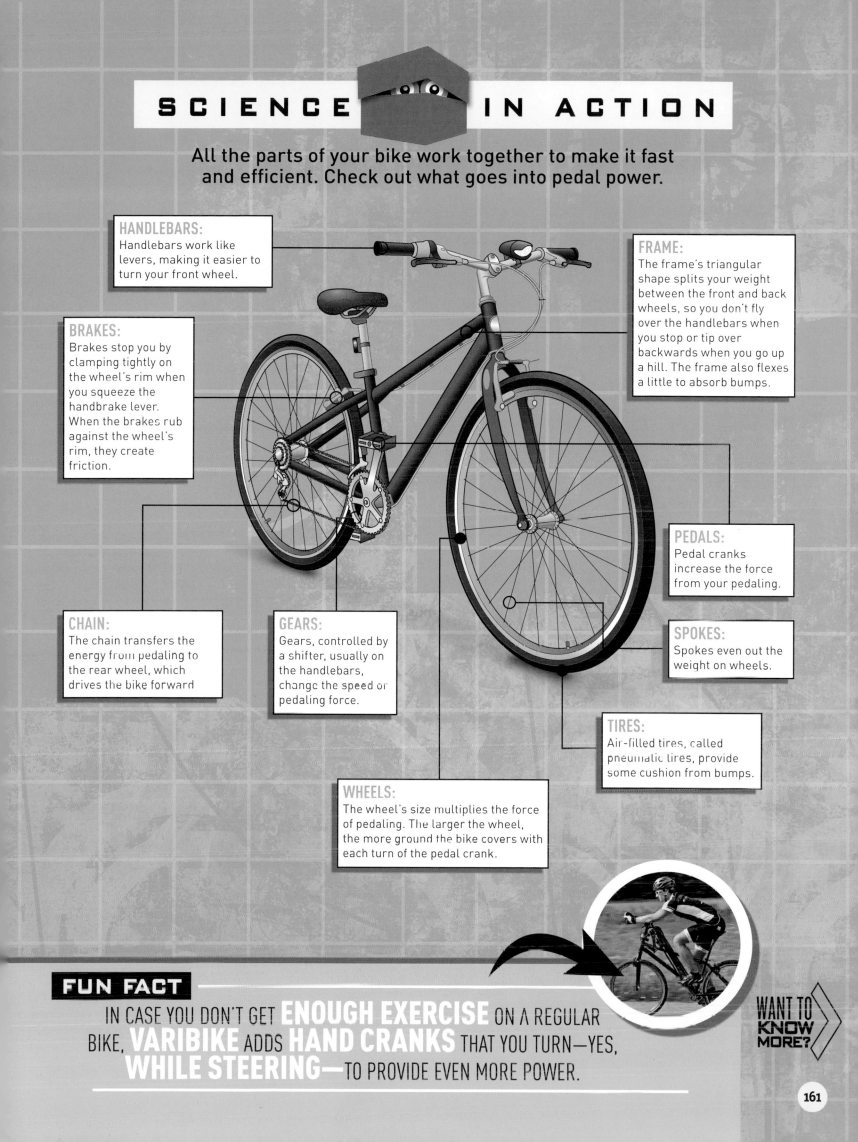

FUN FACT

IN CASE YOU DON'T GET **ENOUGH EXERCISE** ON A REGULAR BIKE, **VARIBIKE** ADDS **HAND CRANKS** THAT YOU TURN—YES, **WHILE STEERING**—TO PROVIDE EVEN MORE POWER.

WANT TO KNOW MORE?

TELL ME MORE

KICKING IT INTO GEAR

If you've ever had to bike up a steep hill, you've probably thanked your bike's gears. Gears are round, toothed wheels that work together to help us generate more power or speed.

A typical bike can have anywhere between 3 and 33 gears. They take the power you create when you pedal and they move it, with the help of a chain, to the bike's back wheel.

The gears are stacked like a sideways wedding cake. When you shift gears, a part called a derailleur moves the chain from one gear to another. If you want to go faster, choose a gear that turns the back wheel many times for each turn of your pedals. If you want to climb a steep hill, shift to a gear that turns the back wheel more slowly but with more force as you pedal.

WHAT A DRAG

The main thing holding a bike back is resistance. Unfortunately, there's more than one kind. Have you noticed that the sides of your bike's tires bulge out a little where the tire hits the ground? Look closely and you'll see that the middle of the tire is a little squashed in, too. As your bike moves, different parts of the tire get squashed or bulge, then regain their shape.

All that squashing and bulging uses energy. It's called rolling resistance. When you strain to pedal up a steep hill, you also battle gravity, the force that keeps us on Earth. And if you're really fast on your bike, you know that air resistance, which pushes against you, is a real drag, too.

WHAT TO DO?

Bikes and cyclists have different ways of dealing with resistance, but nothing works perfectly. Shifting to a lower gear helps you deal with gravity. Cyclists with racing bikes have really skinny tires to reduce rolling resistance, but your best bet is to keep your tires fully inflated so they're harder to squash. If you want to reduce air resistance, tuck your body (bend forward at waist), when going fast. You can also wear tight-fitting clothing, which doesn't catch as much wind.

TRY THIS!

You can compare how far your back wheel goes in different gears. Get someone to help hold your back wheel up. Either mark your back tire (with chalk or tape) or turn the wheel so the air valve is straight up. Start in low gear. Turn your pedal one full revolution and count how many times your wheel went around. Do the same in high gear. If you don't have a bike handy, try rolls of transparent and masking tape! Loop the masking tape roll over your hand and hold the transparent tape right next to it. Mark a dot on the side of each roll at the top. Grab the ends of both tapes and pull until the masking tape's dot travels all the way around once. Did you notice that the transparent tape's dot went farther? The smaller gear has to turn more times to keep up.

FUN FACTS

● Need to cool down on your ride? The Spruzza company makes **a mister** that attaches to your handlebars.

● Some bikes **fold in half.** They're popular with people who live in small apartments or who ride part of the way to work on a train or subway.

SPEEDING UP

Pedaling fast isn't the only way to make a bike speed up. You can also make your bike cover more ground with each turn of the pedal. That's the job of gears. Gear up to see how they work.

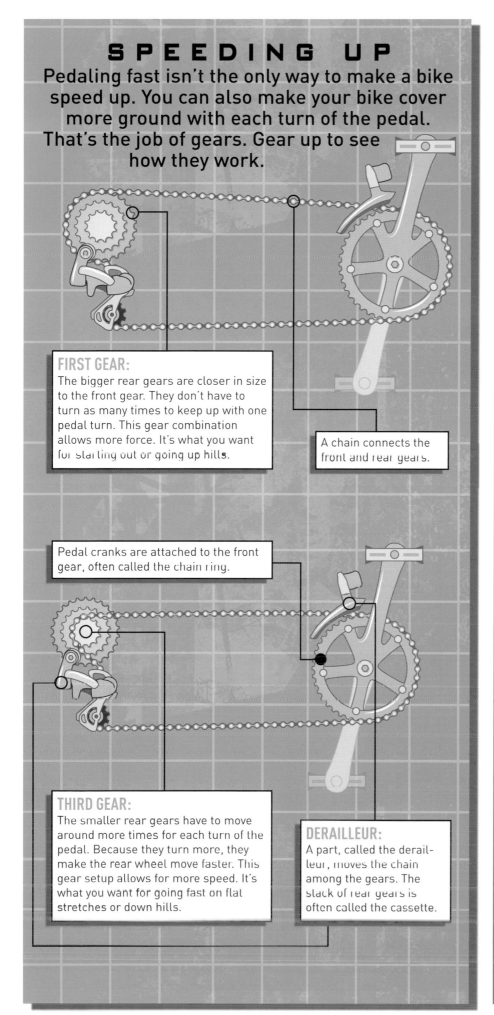

FIRST GEAR:
The bigger rear gears are closer in size to the front gear. They don't have to turn as many times to keep up with one pedal turn. This gear combination allows more force. It's what you want for starting out or going up hills.

A chain connects the front and rear gears.

Pedal cranks are attached to the front gear, often called the chain ring.

THIRD GEAR:
The smaller rear gears have to move around more times for each turn of the pedal. Because they turn more, they make the rear wheel move faster. This gear setup allows for more speed. It's what you want for going fast on flat stretches or down hills.

DERAILLEUR:
A part, called the derailleur, moves the chain among the gears. The stack of rear gears is often called the cassette.

Whoa ... SLOW DOWN! A Closer Look at Gears

Gears are simple—simple machines. Simple machines are basic devices that apply forces and make them bigger. They take something we do, like pedaling, and make it do more. Gears either increase our bike's speed or its power. To go fast, you want a smaller gear on the back wheel, so it has to spin around more times to keep up with your pedaling. That turns the back wheel more frequently, pushing you forward faster. To get up a steep hill more easily, you want to increase your power by using a larger gear on the back wheel. It won't turn as far with each crank of your pedal, but it'll do so with more power to help you conquer that hill. But what if you want to speed up a steep hill without working too hard? Sorry. Gears can't increase both speed and force at the same time. There's always a trade-off. (It's a scientific law! You can only convert energy from one form to another. You can't create it out of nothing.) So, when gears give you more speed, they have to give you less force—but you might not notice if you're already zipping down the road. The reverse is true, too. If gears give you more force, they give you less speed. That's why you have to pedal like crazy to creep up a steep hill in low gear.

TALES FROM THE LAB

GETTING ROLLING:
THE EVOLUTION OF THE BICYCLE

There's a famous saying by the brilliant 17th-century English physicist and mathematician Sir Isaac Newton: "If I have seen a little further, it is by standing on the shoulders of giants." He wasn't talking about a strange type of piggyback ride. He meant that you make progress by building on others' work. That's the story of today's bicycle. It was "invented" over a century. People kept improving on earlier models—and they're not done yet. Check out some highlights of bicycle history.

1817: The "running machine" (or draisine) is the first two-wheeler. Riders push it with their feet and steer. (Few dare to actually lift their feet.) It's faster than walking, but not exactly a speedster.

1863-64: The velocipede ("fast foot" in Latin) adds pedals to the front wheel so riders can go faster. But its heavy frame and wheels—often iron—make for a bumpy ride. People call it the "bone shaker."

1870s: The "ordinary" (or high-wheeler or penny-farthing) has hard rubber tires for a smoother ride and covers ground faster with its big wheel. But with a high center of gravity, riders often sail over the handlebars when stopping suddenly.

1880s: Women's long skirts force them to ride adult tricycles. Lifting their skirts to straddle a high-wheeler might reveal their stockings—a big no-no. Wearing pants is just as scandalous.

1885: The "safety bicycle" changes cycling forever. It has a low seat, chain-driven back wheel, and same-size wheels, so it's easy to ride. It soon gets gears, so it's also zippy. But it still has solid rubber tires. Ouch.

1888: Air-filled, or pneumatic, tires give bikes a much more comfortable ride. A cycling craze starts in both Europe and America.

1890s: Women ditch their skirts for bicycle bloomers—puffy pants that gather together below their knees—and hop on bikes. The biking craze helps advance the cause of women's rights.

1920s: With the American biking craze over, thanks to cars, bicycle makers need new customers. Kids! Kids' bikes, often styled like motorcycles, burst onto the scene.

1960s: A new bicycle boom takes off. Many American riders pedal off on new "English 3-speed" models, but it's the ten-speed "racing bike" that dominates the roads.

1970s: What if you don't want to stay on roads? Cyclists near San Francisco, California, U.S.A., adapt cruiser bikes with extra big "balloon" tires for off-road riding. The mountain bike is born.

THE NICKNAME OF THE "ORDINARY" BIKE—**"PENNY-FARTHING"**—COMES FROM ITS WHEELS' RESEMBLANCE TO TWO OLD **ENGLISH COINS,** A PENNY AND THE MUCH SMALLER FARTHING.

AIR-FILLED BIKE TIRES WERE INVENTED BY A **SCOTTISH VETERINARIAN,** JOHN BOYD DUNLOP, WHO WANTED HIS SON TO HAVE **A CUSHIER RIDE.** THE ELDER DUNLOP THEN STARTED A TIRE COMPANY.

An 1892 advertisement for The Tourist bicycle

Make It BETTER!

Most cities aren't the best places to ride a bike. Bike lanes (if they exist) are usually very narrow and right next to busy traffic. And where do you lock up your bike when you get where you're going, anyway? There aren't nearly enough spaces.

Recently, some cities have made great efforts to become more bike-friendly—encouraging commuters and travelers to use less fuel and more pedal power. They've made more bike lanes, given bikes more of the road, and even created buffers between bikes and cars. Think about your neighborhood. Is it bike-friendly? Imagine you're a city planner. Take some paper and map out your city or neighborhood. What would you change to make it a better place to ride a bike? Or start from scratch and design a new city built just for people who love their bikes!

BACK ON TRACK

How do TRAINS work?

Check It Out!

From steam engines billowing smoke to maglev trains gliding silently over a magnetic field at 200 to 300 miles an hour (322 to 483 km/h), trains are marvels of innovation. They combine power, speed, and versatility in one very long package. Let's track how they work.

How fast can trains go **?**

Does the engineer really drive the train **?**

How do tracks work **?**

JUST THE FACTS

How Does a Train Chug Along?

It takes more than an engine to make a train. It takes an entire system of tracks, signals, and switches to get a train to its destination. The power behind a train is usually a locomotive—sometimes several, if the train is long and heavy. It pulls (or pushes) specially designed cars that carry everything from people to heavy machinery. Inside the locomotive, a train operator (often called an engineer) controls the speed of the train and whether it stops or backs up. But the tracks control where the trains go, and the railway system needs to set switches to move a train from one track to another. Just like on roads, there's traffic on the railways. Signals along the tracks tell the train operator what's up ahead and whether the train needs to slow down or stop.

LOCOMOTIVE:
Locomotives power the train by turning fuel into motion. Diesels pull the heavy freight trains in the United States, but some trains run on electrical power. The steam engines that puffed along tracks in the past now run only on special scenic routes for tourists.

Changing Directions

When trains need to move to a different track, they use switches to get them there. At a switch, the track divides into two. One set of tracks usually continues straight, and a second curves off to the side. The inside rails of both sets are linked together so they can move from side to side. If they're pulled to the right, they close off the tracks to the right and open the path to the left. The switch can be controlled by an electric motor far away or by a nearby hand-operated lever.

In 2015, a Japanese **MAGLEV TRAIN,** which uses magnetic forces to carry the train, hit a record speed of 375 miles an hour (603.5 km/h)—some 17 miles an hour (27 km/h) faster than France's super-high-speed TGV.

FUN FACT

IN EARLY U.S. RAILROADS, THE **DISTANCE BETWEEN** TRACKS, CALLED ITS GAUGE, WAS NOT CONSISTENT. THAT WAS A BIG PROBLEM UNTIL THE END OF THE 1800s WHEN ALL THE U.S. RAILROADS USED THE SAME GAUGE.

IN FOR THE LONG HAUL

Almost anything can be moved by rail.
See how freight trains handle their jobs.

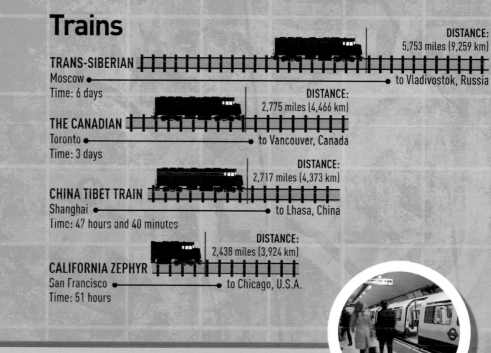

FLAT CAR:
Flat cars carry large objects, like construction equipment, that won't fit inside containers or boxcars.

TANKER:
A tanker holds liquids, such as chemicals.

HOPPER:
A hopper is an open-topped car that usually carries coal or other minerals.

SIGNALS:
Signals along the tracks let the train operators know what's ahead and whether they should keep going fast or slow down.

BOXCAR:
A boxcar carries cargo, such as crates and other goods, which are loaded through sliding doors on the boxcar's sides.

RAILS:
A pair of rails, sitting on railroad ties, guides the train. Their smooth steel reduces the friction of the wheels running on them, and that helps the train use less energy.

CONTAINER CAR:
A container is filled with goods at another location. The containers can be loaded onto trains from ships or transferred from trains to trailers pulled by trucks.

ALL ABOARD!

Hope you like **road trips**—or "track" trips—because these are some long rides! In fact, they're some of the **longest train rides** in the world. These tracks span countries and continents and pass breathtaking views, all while getting passengers where they need to go.

Trains

TRANS-SIBERIAN
Moscow
Time: 6 days
to Vladivostok, Russia
DISTANCE:
5,753 miles (9,259 km)

THE CANADIAN
Toronto
Time: 3 days
to Vancouver, Canada
DISTANCE:
2,775 miles (4,466 km)

CHINA TIBET TRAIN
Shanghai
Time: 47 hours and 40 minutes
to Lhasa, China
DISTANCE:
2,717 miles (4,373 km)

CALIFORNIA ZEPHYR
San Francisco
Time: 51 hours
to Chicago, U.S.A.
DISTANCE:
2,438 miles (3,924 km)

FUN FACT
THE LONDON **UNDERGROUND** OPENED IN 1863. ITS FIRST TRAINS WERE **STEAM-POWERED,** AND THE SMOKE IN THE ENCLOSED TUNNELS MADE PASSENGERS GAG. THE TUBE, AS IT'S COMMONLY CALLED, NOW CARRIES 1.26 BILLION PASSENGERS A YEAR.

WANT TO KNOW MORE?

TELL ME MORE

WHEN IS A DIESEL LOCOMOTIVE NOT A DIESEL?

Many of today's diesel engines are actually more like hybrid engines. They combine two types of power, in this case diesel and electrical.

These locomotives have a large diesel engine that powers an electrical generator. The electricity produced by the generator travels down to "traction motors," one on each of the twelve wheels on a locomotive. These motors turn the wheels and send the train traveling down the rail.

Very little of each wheel actually is in contact with the rail at any given moment—only about a fingernail's width. That means there's very little friction created by the wheels rubbing against the rails. On top of that, multiple locomotives in one train "talk" to each other about the best way to use their combined power. All these things means that these locomotives can do their job using less energy. A modern hybrid diesel locomotive can move one ton of freight 479 miles (770 km) on one gallon (3.8 L) of diesel fuel.

SPEED LIMITS

Fast engines are great, but it's really the tracks that matter. When setting train speed limits, engineers look at how curvy a track is, what shape it's in, whether there are railroad crossings on the line, and whether signals control the track.

CURVY FORCES

When a train is on straight tracks, its center of gravity—the point where its weight is evenly distributed and it's in balance—is directly over its wheels. When a train goes around a curve, it encounters centrifugal force. Centrifugal force makes something that's going around a circular path move out, away from the center of its path. If the train is too light, its speed too high, and the curve too sharp, the train is no longer balanced and centrifugal force can cause it to tip off the rails.

FUN FACTS

● **Underground rail systems,** or **subways,** move millions of people every day. They are amazing feats of engineering. The world's first subway systems, like those in London, Paris, and New York, were dug by hand. Today, massive **tunnel-boring machines,** which stand several stories tall, cut through bedrock, soil, and debris. Sometimes cities build new subways by digging **deep trenches,** building roofs over the new rail systems, and covering them back up with dirt.

● A **miniature railroad** exhibit at **Miniatur Wunderland,** in Germany, features some **930 trains** running on more than 8 miles (13 km) of track. It's rivaled by the Northlandz model railroad in New Jersey, U.S.A., which has the same length of track but about **100 trains.** Northlandz was built by one man, Bruce Williams Zaccagnino.

● The New York subway has **469 stations,** more than any other system in the world. More than **4.5 million people** ride it **every weekday.**

POWERHOUSE

Most of today's "diesel" engines actually run on both diesel fuel and electricity. But the newest hybrid locomotives also use special technology to use even less energy. Climb on board to see how they work.

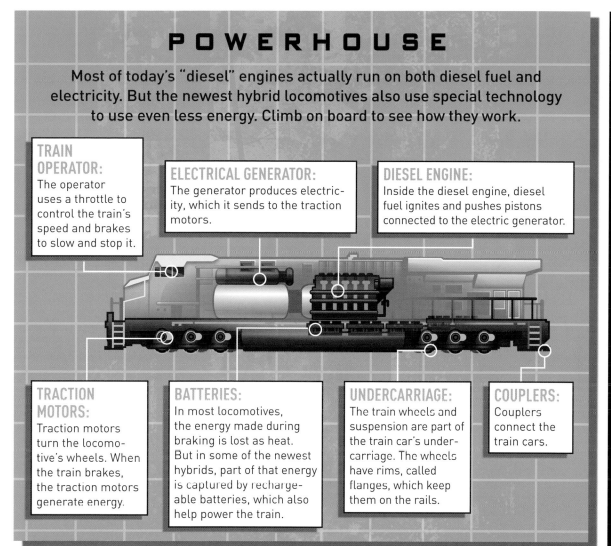

TRAIN OPERATOR: The operator uses a throttle to control the train's speed and brakes to slow and stop it.

ELECTRICAL GENERATOR: The generator produces electricity, which it sends to the traction motors.

DIESEL ENGINE: Inside the diesel engine, diesel fuel ignites and pushes pistons connected to the electric generator.

TRACTION MOTORS: Traction motors turn the locomotive's wheels. When the train brakes, the traction motors generate energy.

BATTERIES: In most locomotives, the energy made during braking is lost as heat. But in some of the newest hybrids, part of that energy is captured by rechargeable batteries, which also help power the train.

UNDERCARRIAGE: The train wheels and suspension are part of the train car's undercarriage. The wheels have rims, called flanges, which keep them on the rails.

COUPLERS: Couplers connect the train cars.

TRY THIS!
Why is a shift of center of gravity so important for trains? You can try it yourself. If you stand up and lean to the side, you may fall over. People are a little top-heavy. We have a center of gravity a bit above our waists. When you stand up straight, your center of gravity is safely over your feet. But when you lean, where is it? Your center of gravity **shifts to the side** and isn't above your feet anymore. It throws you off balance.

How Things Worked

Diesel locomotives may rule the rails now, but it was the steam engine that revolutionized the world. From the early 1800s through the mid-1900s, steam locomotives transformed transportation and knitted together the sprawling United States. Goods no longer had to travel on canals and other waterways, and people could travel fast and far without bumping along in horse-pulled wagons. So how did this marvelous invention work? A steam locomotive burns coal, wood, or oil to boil water into steam. The steam from the boiler travels through a pipe and moves a piston back and forth. The piston connects to a crank and rod that turn the wheels. That *chug-chug* you hear? It's from the piston moving back and forth, which also sends puffs of steam up the smokestack along with smoke from the fire. But steamies weren't the first vehicles to chug along tracks. More than 2,000 years ago, the ancient Egyptians, Babylonians, and Greeks built stone "wagonways" with ruts that forced horse-pulled carts to go along a path. That technology wasn't revived until the 1500s and 1600s, when Europeans used wagonways for hand propelled and horse-pulled transportation. Once steam locomotives were invented, they took over the rails. But steam power had some early competition. In the early and mid-1850s, some trains were pulled by horses and others were even powered by wind. One locomotive carried horses that walked on treadmills to power the wheels. That's serious horsepower!

171

KEEPING STEP

How does an ESCALATOR keep us moving along?

Check It Out!

When the first escalator was made, people didn't quite know what to make of it—and neither did its creator. It ended up as a ride in an amusement park. Since that humble beginning, escalators have become one of largest machines people use on a regular basis. Step up your knowledge about an escalator's ups and downs.

Where do the steps go after they reach the end ?

Why do the steps have grooves ?

How do the steps fold down at the top and bottom ?

JUST THE FACTS

Moving Experience

Escalators are masters at moving a lot of people quickly up and down—even more so than elevators, as long as it's a short distance. You might think something this clever would require an elaborate design and complicated parts, but an escalator is really quite simple. It's basically a big, tilted conveyor belt with a twist at the end—literally—so the steps can flatten. Chains looped around gears do the heavy lifting, and an electric motor powers the whole system. All the machinery hides underground, so it looks as simple as it is to ride.

What a Ride!

The first working escalator was the "inclined elevator" invented by Jesse Reno in 1891. It was a hit—initially as an amusement-park ride at New York City's Coney Island. A decade later, Reno wanted to add seats to the handrail, but the design never took off. Men could have straddled the conveyor, but ladies would have been expected to choose a more refined "sidesaddle" position.

ESCALATOR vs. ELEVATOR

Imagine you're designing a **three-story hotel.** What are you going to put in the lobby—**escalators or elevators?**

A hypothetical building three floors tall

would require ...

2 ESCALATORS:
(running 12 hours a day) using **75,000 kWh/yr** of electricity. But guests don't have to wait.

-OR-

5 ELEVATORS:
(including lighting) using **68,000 kWh/yr** of electricity. But guests have to wait.

As a comparison, the average American home consumes 11,040 kWh/yr.

Advanced escalators that idle when not in use can cut electricity use by about 28%.

TRY THIS!

You can see how an escalator's steps rise—without even traveling to the shopping mall. Get a black binder clip and take off its handles. (You may need a grown-up's help.) Now your binder clip is the same shape as an escalator step. Hang it on something skinny, like a straightened paper clip, so it can swing freely. Do you see how it hangs at an angle? That's like a real escalator step right before it emerges at the bottom of an escalator. To become a flat surface that you can stand on, the step needs something to push it up from below. A real escalator uses a special track to do that job, but you can push the bottom of your "step" up with anything you like. Sliding it up against a slanted ruler works great.

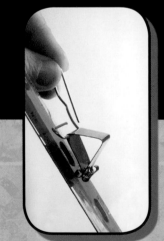

One of an escalator's neatest tricks is making the steps rise up when you need them, but then fold flat at the end of the ride. How does it do this? Each step is wedge-shaped. Its top wheels, near its pointy part, roll along one track. Its lower wheels roll along a second track. When the steps need to be flat, the second track dips down lower so the back of the step has room to drop down. When the step needs to pop up, the second track lifts it.

TAKING IT A STEP AT A TIME

An escalator is like a big conveyor belt tilted at an incline. It's a big machine, but a simple solution for moving a lot of people up and down in a little time. Take a look.

STEPS:
Each step has two sets of wheels, which roll along separate tracks. The wheels near the top of the step are connected to the chains. The other wheels follow along on a second track.

HANDRAIL:
The rubber handrails are designed to move at the same speed as the steps, so riders can hold them for safety.

DRIVE GEAR:
The drive gears at the top turn a pair of chains, which also attach to the gears at the bottom. The chains pull the steps.

INNER RAIL/TRACK:
The tracks bend to level off at the top and bottom, so the steps flatten into platforms. The grooves in the steps make sure the steps fit together, like puzzle pieces, when flat.

ELECTRIC MOTOR:
An electric motor provides the power that moves the steps and the handrails.

HANDRAIL DRIVE:
The gears that turn the steps also turn the handrails.

RAIL/TRACK FOR LOWER WHEELS:
The track for the lower wheels either lifts the steps to carry you up and down or lets them drop to flatten out.

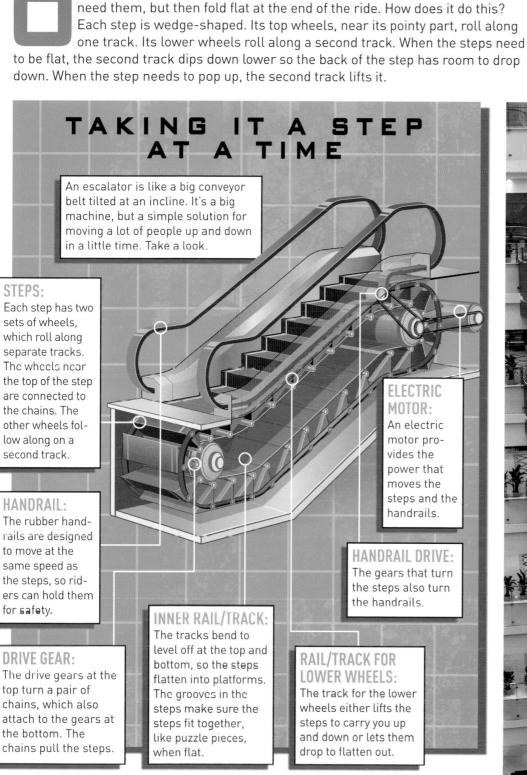

FUN FACT

● The **world's first** working **spiral escalator** was installed in **Osaka, Japan,** in 1985.

DEEP DIVER

How does a SUBMARINE move underwater?

Check It Out!

Submarines slip underwater. They move along quietly, playing a high-stakes game of hide-and-seek. Those long cylinder-shaped vessels can dive underwater and stay there for weeks or even months. Have you ever wondered what it would be like to be on a sub? Take a deep breath. We're diving into the details of how a nuclear submarine works.

How do submarines dive down **?**

How do they know where they're going **?**

How do sailors get enough air to breathe **?**

JUST THE FACTS

Cruising in the Depths

It takes more to get a boat to dive and cruise underwater than making it a watertight tube (though that certainly helps). A submarine's hull, its metal outside, doesn't just keep water out. It also prevents the sub from being crushed by water pressure when it's deep in the sea. Unlike most ships, a sub has a two-layered hull. Its outer hull is waterproof. Its inner hull, the pressure hull, is much stronger to withstand water pressure. Between the two hulls are spaces, called ballast tanks, which can be filled with either air or water. When the submarine wants to dive, it fills the ballast tanks with water. When it wants to rise to the surface, it fills them with air.

NUCLEAR SUBMARINES can go faster than **25 KNOTS** (more than 29 miles or 46 km an hour) and dive deeper than **800 FEET** (244 m).

THAT'S SO DEEP

Submarines aren't the only things you can find **diving beneath the ocean's surface.** Humans and other animals can go deep, with and without the help of technology. Just see for yourself!

10 FEET (3 M): The deep end of an average swimming pool

115 FEET (35 M): Average inshore depth of the Great Barrier Reef

MORE THAN 800 FEET (244 M): The depth that a U.S. Navy submarine goes

831 FEET (253.2 M): Herbert Nitsch, June 6, 2012, free dive off Santorini, Greece

1,850 FEET (565 M): Dive depth of an emperor penguin

6.83 MILES (11 KM): Challenger Deep, the Mariana Trench's lowest point

NEARLY REACHED BY James Cameron, March 26, 2012, in a custom-built submersible. He reached a depth of 35,686 ft (10.88 km)

FUN FACT

SHIPS MEASURE THEIR SPEED IN **"KNOTS,"** A TERM DATING BACK TO A TIME WHEN SAILORS MEASURED A SHIP'S SPEED USING A ROPE KNOTTED AT REGULAR INTERVALS AND TIED TO A PIECE OF WOOD.

DIVING IN

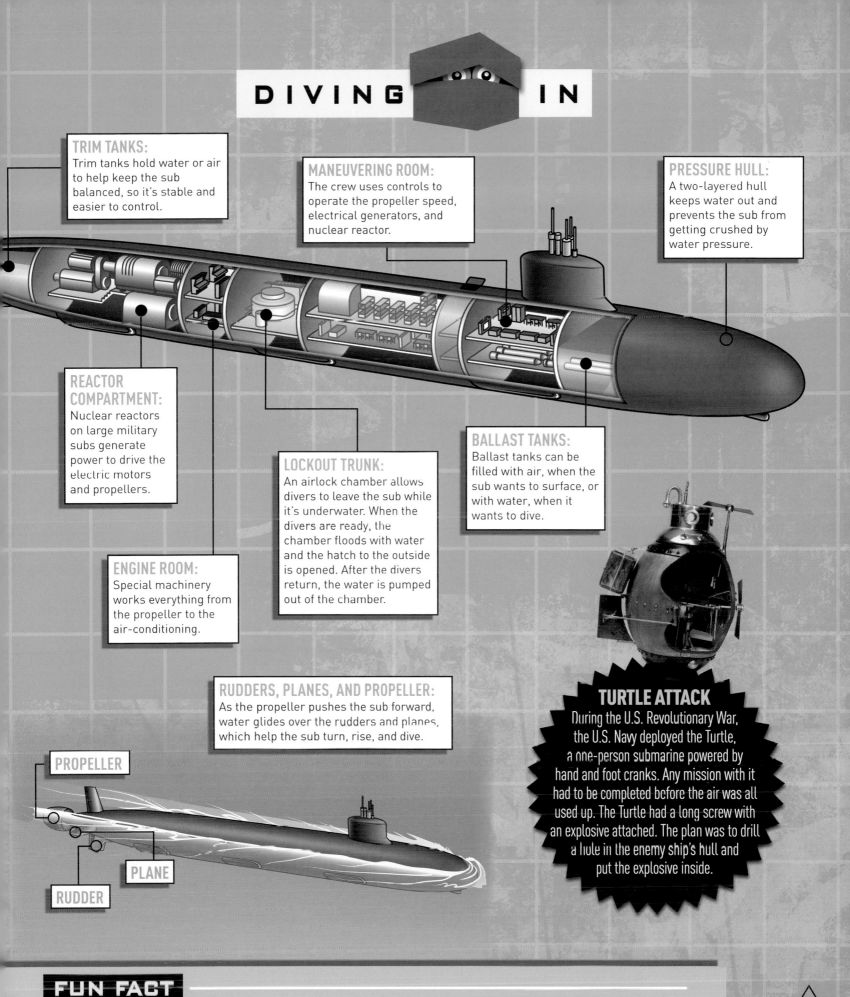

TRIM TANKS:
Trim tanks hold water or air to help keep the sub balanced, so it's stable and easier to control.

MANEUVERING ROOM:
The crew uses controls to operate the propeller speed, electrical generators, and nuclear reactor.

PRESSURE HULL:
A two-layered hull keeps water out and prevents the sub from getting crushed by water pressure.

REACTOR COMPARTMENT:
Nuclear reactors on large military subs generate power to drive the electric motors and propellers.

ENGINE ROOM:
Special machinery works everything from the propeller to the air-conditioning.

LOCKOUT TRUNK:
An airlock chamber allows divers to leave the sub while it's underwater. When the divers are ready, the chamber floods with water and the hatch to the outside is opened. After the divers return, the water is pumped out of the chamber.

BALLAST TANKS:
Ballast tanks can be filled with air, when the sub wants to surface, or with water, when it wants to dive.

RUDDERS, PLANES, AND PROPELLER:
As the propeller pushes the sub forward, water glides over the rudders and planes, which help the sub turn, rise, and dive.

PROPELLER

PLANE

RUDDER

TURTLE ATTACK
During the U.S. Revolutionary War, the U.S. Navy deployed the Turtle, a one-person submarine powered by hand and foot cranks. Any mission with it had to be completed before the air was all used up. The Turtle had a long screw with an explosive attached. The plan was to drill a hole in the enemy ship's hull and put the explosive inside.

FUN FACT
"SUBMARINE" MEANS **"UNDER THE SEA."** THE VESSELS ORIGINALLY WERE CALLED "SUBMARINE BOATS." SAILORS STILL REFER TO THEM AS **"BOATS"** INSTEAD OF "SHIPS." IT'S A TRADITION.

WANT TO KNOW MORE?

TELL ME MORE

FINDING THEIR WAY

Submarines rely on a lot of electronic equipment to navigate underwater. Sonar helps them find out what's nearby. A sub can have active sonar, which sends out sound waves and listens for their echoes, or passive sonar, which only listens.

A global positioning system (GPS) uses satellites to tell the submarine its location. Submarines also have special equipment to receive and send out radio signals and to detect the radar of other craft.

Some submarines have cameras mounted on their masts. Others have periscopes, the viewing tubes that can be raised when the sub is near the surface. But those aren't much help deep in the sea!

LIVING UNDERWATER

A submarine is completely sealed. Water can't get in—and neither can fresh air. So how do the sailors breathe?

Submarines carry tanks of oxygen, but they also do a really cool trick. They make their own oxygen out of water! Have you ever heard water called "H_2O"? That refers to water's molecules—the tiny particles that make it. The O stands for oxygen, and the H stands for hydrogen.

Subs use a special process, called electrolysis, that gets the "O" out of water. Another device cleans the excess carbon dioxide, the stuff we exhale, out of the air. Voilà, air!

And if that's not cool enough, subs have another trick. They can take seawater and purify it so sailors can drink it and take showers.

A special process, called distillation, heats the seawater until it's vapor, which leaves the salt behind. It then cools the vapor back into fresh water.

How Things Worked

People have wanted to explore the ocean depths for centuries. To get there, they dreamed up some seriously strange submersibles!

The first scientific reference to a submarine vessel dates back to 1580. English innkeeper and amateur scientist William Bourne described how to make a boat "goe under the water unto the bottome, and so to come up again at your pleasure." What Bourne figured out—unlike everyone before him—was how a submarine's shape affects its buoyancy. He designed a boat with a waterproofed leather covering whose size could be changed from the inside by turning big screws. If you turned the screws so they pushed the covering out, the boat would puff out and rise. If you turned them the other way, the boat would shrink and sink. He also wanted the boat to have a tall, hollow mast—like a giant straw—to let in air.

Several years later, someone changed his idea so the screws would open and close chambers that could be flooded like ballast tanks.

It wasn't until the 1620s that an inventor made a working submarine, though. Dutchman Cornelius Drebbel designed a way for a submersible boat to move underwater. Drebbel's sub, a decked-over rowboat that probably sloped down in the front, had twelve people manning oars. When they rowed hard enough, they drove the boat just below the water's surface. When they stopped rowing, the boat bobbed back up.

Giovanni Borelli's 1680 design for a submarine

WHERE ARE WE? WHERE ARE WE? WHERE...

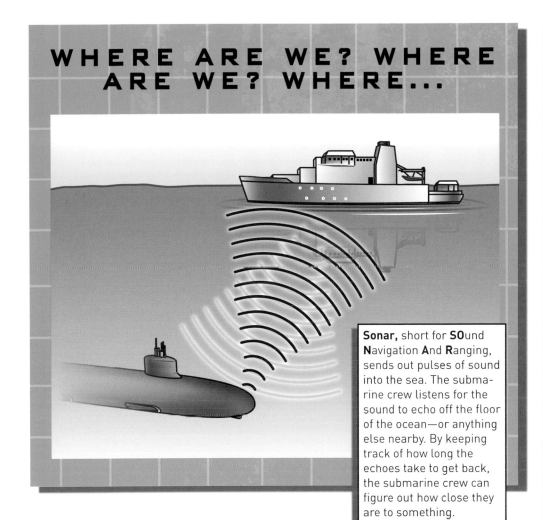

Sonar, short for **SO**und **N**avigation **A**nd **R**anging, sends out pulses of sound into the sea. The submarine crew listens for the sound to echo off the floor of the ocean—or anything else nearby. By keeping track of how long the echoes take to get back, the submarine crew can figure out how close they are to something.

THAT SINKING FEELING

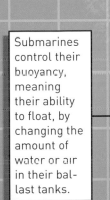

Submarines control their buoyancy, meaning their ability to float, by changing the amount of water or air in their ballast tanks.

When they want to dive, they fill their tanks with water so they get heavier.

When they want to rise, they force air into the tanks. The air pushes the water out of the tanks and back into the ocean. The air in the ballast tanks is a lot lighter than water, so the submarine becomes more buoyant.

WHAT A BLAST!

How do ROCKETS fly into space?

Check It 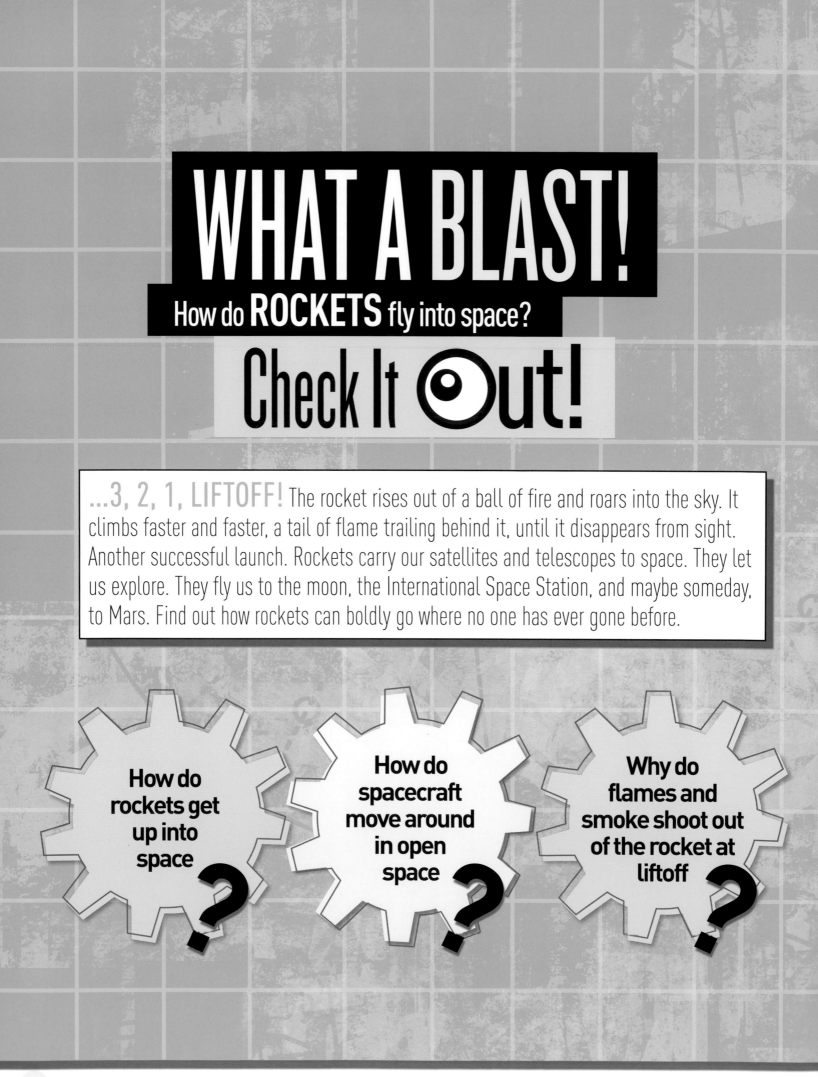ut!

...3, 2, 1, LIFTOFF! The rocket rises out of a ball of fire and roars into the sky. It climbs faster and faster, a tail of flame trailing behind it, until it disappears from sight. Another successful launch. Rockets carry our satellites and telescopes to space. They let us explore. They fly us to the moon, the International Space Station, and maybe someday, to Mars. Find out how rockets can boldly go where no one has ever gone before.

How do rockets get up into space **?**

How do spacecraft move around in open space **?**

Why do flames and smoke shoot out of the rocket at liftoff **?**

JUST THE FACTS

Two-for-One

It's like getting two for the price of one. When you watch a rocket blast off, you're really seeing more than one actual rocket. Most rockets have multiple stages, like two rockets stacked on top of each other. The bottom rocket, called the core stage, has the job of lifting the spacecraft off the launch pad. When it runs out of fuel or reaches a target speed or height, it drops off. The upper rocket continues the journey.

Powering Up

It takes a massive amount of energy to break free of Earth's gravity. On NASA's Space Launch System, for example, four main engines burn 1,500 gallons (5,700 L) of fuel each second. That's like draining a family-size swimming pool in a single minute. It's enough power to keep eight 747 aircraft aloft—but it's still not enough to lift off. Two extra boosters attached to the rocket's sides provide more than three-fourths of the energy at launch. The boosters burn ten tons (about 9 metric tons) of fuel per second. They only fire for two minutes, but in that time they make enough power to run 92,000 houses for an entire day. After they use up their fuel, they drop off, and the main engines continue the push into space. To reach deep space, the rocket needs an upper stage with its own engine.

Easy Sailing

Once a spacecraft reaches open space, it doesn't need to fire its engines. It keeps moving forward, like it's coasting, and then goes into orbit, looping around a planet, moon, or star. If it wants to change direction, go into higher or lower orbit, or head back to Earth, it needs to fire small rockets called thrusters.

FUN FACT

IN THE LATE TENTH CENTURY, THE CHINESE CREATED "FIRE ARROWS," BAMBOO TUBES STUFFED WITH GUNPOWDER AND ATTACHED TO ARROWS. THOSE LED TO THE FIRST ROCKETS, WHICH WERE LIKE FIREWORK MISSILES. THE CHINESE USED THEM IN 1232 TO DEFEND AGAINST AN INVASION.

DESTINATION: MARS

NASA's Orion space capsule can carry a crew deep into space, but it can't get there on its own. Orion needs a boost from the most powerful rocket ever built, NASA's heavy-lift Space Launch System, or SLS.

CORE STAGE/LIQUID FUEL:
The SLS carries enough fuel to produce a lot of thrust, the force that drives the rocket up. Its thrust is 31 times stronger than that of a Boeing 747 jet.

UPPER STAGE/LIQUID FUEL:
After lapping the Earth once, the upper rocket fires to take Orion deeper into space, more than 3,600 miles (5,800 km) above Earth.

SOLID ROCKET BOOSTER:
Two solid rocket boosters provide most of the power for liftoff.

ENGINES:
One RS-25 engine could power 846,591 miles (1,362,456 km) of residential streetlights—a street long enough to go to the moon and back and circle Earth 15 times.

A BRIEF HISTORY OF BLASTING OFF

Space travel has been a **long, _long_ time** coming. Take a look at these major milestones in history to find out how we got to where we are today.

10TH CENTURY
Gunpowder invented in China to fuel rockets for warfare.

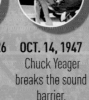

MARCH 16, 1926
Robert Goddard successfully launches first liquid-fueled rocket.

OCT. 14, 1947
Chuck Yeager breaks the sound barrier.

NOV. 3, 1957
The USSR sends the first living passenger, Laika the dog, into space.

JULY 20, 1969
U.S. astronauts Neil Armstrong and Buzz Aldrin become the first men to walk on the moon.

NOV. 20, 1998
The first segment of the International Space Station is launched by Russia.

JAN. 4, 2004
The exploration rover Spirit lands on Mars.

JAN. 19, 2006
NASA's New Horizons launches a rocket to fly by Pluto and its moons.

JULY 23, 2015
Delta IV rocket launches from Cape Canaveral to aid in U.S. military satellite communications.

900 1920 1930 1940 1950 1960 1970 1980 1990 2000 2010 2015

FUN FACT

IN 1899, ROBERT H. GODDARD, ONE OF THE **"FATHERS OF MODERN ROCKETRY,"** WAS INSPIRED TO PURSUE SPACE FLIGHT AFTER HE CLIMBED A CHERRY TREE AND GAZED UP AT THE SKY.

WANT TO KNOW MORE?

PROFILE: Elon Musk

VISIONARY

Elon Musk sees things that most people can't. He sees a future where people drive electric cars powered by the sun's rays and ride trains that go faster than jets. He sees people traveling to Mars and building a livable colony there.

Is he just dreaming? That's what many people thought. They laughed at his ideas.

That is, until Elon launched a rocket to the International Space Station and built an all-electric car that does everything a regular car can do—only better.

Elon didn't stop there. He started working on ways to harness solar energy and dreamed up a Hyperloop train that would zip through a giant tube at incredible speeds. He even started a school.

People started calling Elon the real-life Tony Stark, the billionaire genius inventor from the Iron Man comics.

Elon was used to being laughed at, but he never dreamed he'd be compared to Iron Man.

A SURVIVOR
Growing up in South Africa, Elon had a rough life. At school, he stood out both for his smarts and his small size—and he was bullied for it.

"I was this little bookwormy kid, and probably a little bit of a smart aleck, so this was a recipe for disaster," he says. "So I just read a lot of books and tried to stay out of people's way during school."

From the moment he woke up until he went to sleep, he read— comic books, science fiction,

fantasy, whatever. "At one point I ran out of books and started reading the encyclopedia."

He learned a lot on his own. When he was ten, he bought a computer and taught himself how to program it by reading books. At twelve, he sold his first video game, a space game called Blastar.

As he grew up, he decided to move to the United States. Cool technology was being developed there, especially in California's Silicon Valley, and he wanted to be part of it.

FOCUSED ON THE FUTURE
Elon decided that the Internet, sustainable energy, and space exploration would shape our future.

He studied physics and economics in college, and then started graduate school. But he was afraid that during the years he'd be working on a Ph.D., he'd miss his chance to be part of the Internet boom. So he left graduate school after only two days and started various Internet businesses.

Elon was really successful. He made enough money from his Internet businesses to buy a private island somewhere and not work another day in his life. But that's not Elon.

"For me it was never about money, but solving problems for the future of humanity," he says.

Elon never planned to make rockets or cars. But when it looked like the U.S. space program wasn't pushing into deep

space and carmakers weren't designing electric cars fast enough, Elon stepped in.

He felt he had to. The way he sees it, our future depends on changing the way we use energy

> ❝ THE HEROES OF THE BOOKS I READ ALWAYS FELT A DUTY TO SAVE THE WORLD. ❞

and expanding our knowledge of the universe. And if it takes Elon to make that happen, he's up for it.

"The heroes of the books I read, *The Lord of the Rings* and the *Foundation* series, always felt a duty to save the world," he says. He did, too.

He poured all his money into his rocket company, SpaceX, and his electric-car company, Tesla. It was a rocky start. His first three rockets failed, and the early Teslas had problems. Elon and his companies almost went broke.

But he didn't give up.

"If something's important enough, then you do it even though the risk of failure is high."

Today, Elon's companies are pioneers in space exploration and electric-car design, and Elon's trying to change how the world uses energy. He wants to harness the colossal energy of the sun, storing it in batteries in our homes, so we can stop drilling for oil and digging up coal.

It's another big idea. Only this time, hardly anyone's laughing at Elon.

ELON LEARNED HOW TO **DESIGN ROCKETS** BY READING BOOKS.

SPACEX

THE **HYPERLOOP TRAIN,** AS ENVISIONED BY ELON, COULD TRAVEL 800 MILES AN HOUR (1,287 KM/H). IT WOULD WORK BY CREATING A PARTIAL VACUUM INSIDE A TUBE AND **GUIDING TRAIN PODS** ALONG IT USING MAGNETS. THE WHOLE SYSTEM WOULD BE SOLAR POWERED.

ELON **INSPIRED** ACTOR ROBERT DOWNEY, JR., IN HOW TO PORTRAY BILLIONAIRE GENIUS INVENTOR TONY STARK IN THE **IRON MAN MOVIES.**

HITTING THE ROAD

How does a HYBRID CAR work?

Check It Out!

What do you get when you combine a gasoline engine and an electric motor in a car? A hybrid, of course. But not just that. You also get a much more efficient vehicle, meaning it moves around using less energy and creating less pollution. That's good for our environment, our health, and our wallets. So how do these two powerhouses work together? Fasten your seat belt, because we're about to find out.

Where do hybrids get their energy?

Do you have to plug in hybrids to charge them?

Why do hybrids still have gasoline engines?

JUST THE FACTS

The world's first hybrid car, the Lohner-Porsche Mixte.

Teamwork

In a hybrid, a gasoline engine and an electric motor work together to zip you around town using the least amount of energy possible. There are different ways of doing this, but here's how it often works. The gasoline engine provides most of the vehicle's power, especially when cruising along at highway speeds. The electric motor takes over in the stop-and-go driving on city streets. Both kick in to provide an extra boost when needed, like when you need to accelerate quickly or pass another car. When a hybrid stops, even if it's only at a red light, both the gasoline engine and the electric motor shut off so they don't waste energy.

Choices, Choices

Hybrids work lots of different ways. Some hybrids need to be plugged in to recharge the battery. Others get all the charge they need from driving around. But those aren't the only differences. In some hybrids, the gasoline engine and electric motor both send power to the wheels. In others, the motor powers the car, but it gets its energy from the engine. Full hybrids have electric motors strong enough to power the car independently. But in "mild hybrids," the electric motor is too small to do the job by itself. That's a lot of different technologies—and it doesn't even include the all-electric cars!

Hybrid cars may seem like a **NEW INNOVATION,** but they date back to **1900**. The Lohner-Porsche Mixte, made in Austria, zipped along on power from an electric motor, charged by a gasoline engine. The Mixte was made until 1915, but it was too expensive to compete with the cheaper gasoline-powered cars on the market.

SOARING SUSTAINABLY

Who says green vehicles have to stay on land? Although **hybrid-electric** and **electric aircraft** aren't as commonplace as hybrid cars, researchers are working on taking hybrids to new heights.

On August 20, 2014, NASA tested its hybrid-electric vertical takeoff airplane in hopes of one day replacing gas-guzzling helicopters. The drawback? It only had a wingspan of 10 feet (3 m).

An electric helicopter designed by Sikorsky's Project Firefly is 3x as efficient as its gas-engine counterparts.

In 2014, researchers from the University of Cambridge, U.K., tested a hybrid plane that uses about 30 percent less fuel than standard planes.

FUN FACT

HOW ABOUT A **HUMAN-ELECTRIC HYBRID?** IN EUROPE, THE TWIKE, A THREE-WHEELED TWO-SEATER VEHICLE, COMBINES AN ELECTRIC MOTOR AND PEDAL POWER. IT CAN ZIP ALONG AT SPEEDS UP TO **53 MILES AN HOUR** (85 KM/H).

M I X I N G   IT UP

A hybrid car uses both a gasoline-powered engine and an electric motor to power a car. Let's see how they pair up to provide your ride.

BATTERY:
The battery, which is much larger than the one in regular cars, helps power the car and stores energy.

ELECTRIC MOTOR:
The electric motor kicks in when the gasoline engine needs help. It also generates energy during braking and by converting some of the gasoline engine's power.

TRANSMISSION:
The transmission system uses the power to move the car.

GAS ENGINE:
The gasoline engine powers the car when it's cruising along at highway speeds. It also generates energy to store in the battery.

FUN FACT

ALMOST EVERY **FIFTH NEW CAR** BOUGHT IN JAPAN **IS A HYBRID.** THAT MAKES JAPAN THE **WORLD LEADER** IN HYBRID CAR OWNERSHIP.

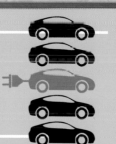

WANT TO **KNOW MORE?**

STOPPING TO GO

When you hit the brakes in a regular car, a lot of energy is wasted. Some of the car's kinetic energy, the energy moving it forward, escapes as heat from the friction of the brakes clamping down on the wheels. But a hybrid captures the car's kinetic energy and reuses it to charge its batteries.

It manages this feat with a system called regenerative braking. When a hybrid slows down or goes downhill, its electric motor stops pushing the car. In fact, the electric motor lets the wheels turn it backwards, so it works like a generator, making electricity instead of using it. The wheels' effort to turn the motor also slows down the car. If they need more help, regular brakes kick in.

TRY THIS!

If your bike has hand brakes, try this test the next time you go for a ride. Before you start moving, touch the rubber brake pads to see how warm they are. Now ride fast and brake to a quick and full stop. Check the brake pads again. They should be warmer, thanks to the friction of the pads rubbing on the wheel. Now go wash your hands—those brake pads were dirty. (If you rather not get your hands dirty to perform this experiment, just rub them together really fast. That warmth you feel is thanks to friction.)

Break pads

FUN FACTS

● Many carmakers produced hybrids in the **early 1900s,** but cheap gasoline and innovations in gasoline-powered engines and car production soon made gasoline-powered cars **cheaper** and more popular.

● The Toyota Prius, the first **mass-produced hybrid** car, hit the roads in Japan in 1997. Three years later, it was on sale around the world. It's still the world's best-selling hybrid car.

● Cars aren't the only vehicles with hybrid engines. **Locomotives** have used them for years, as have **submarines.**

PISTON POWER

The powerhouse of a gasoline engine is the cylinder, where the fuel ignites and creates the energy that drives the car forward. Inside the cylinder is a piston attached to an axle called the crankshaft. The crankshaft powers the gears that turn the car's wheels. Let's peer inside a cylinder to see what really drives the car.

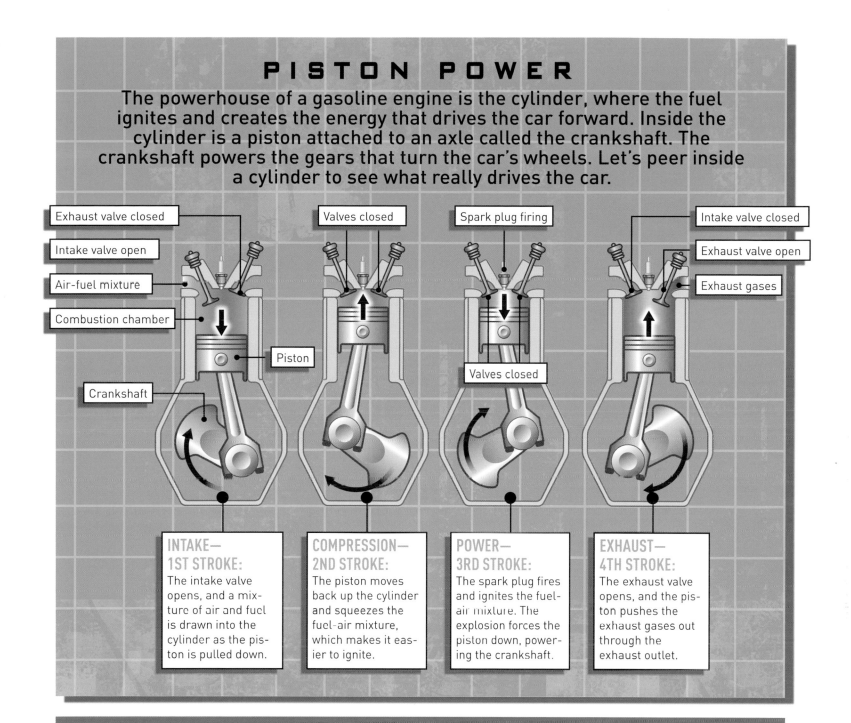

Exhaust valve closed

Intake valve open

Air-fuel mixture

Combustion chamber

Piston

Crankshaft

Valves closed

Spark plug firing

Valves closed

Intake valve closed

Exhaust valve open

Exhaust gases

INTAKE— 1ST STROKE:
The intake valve opens, and a mixture of air and fuel is drawn into the cylinder as the piston is pulled down.

COMPRESSION— 2ND STROKE:
The piston moves back up the cylinder and squeezes the fuel-air mixture, which makes it easier to ignite.

POWER— 3RD STROKE:
The spark plug fires and ignites the fuel-air mixture. The explosion forces the piston down, powering the crankshaft.

EXHAUST— 4TH STROKE:
The exhaust valve opens, and the piston pushes the exhaust gases out through the exhaust outlet.

Whoa ... SLOW DOWN! A Closer Look at Engines and Motors

Hybrid cars have both an engine and a motor. And sometimes the motor acts like a generator (when the car brakes). Engines, motors, generators ... what's the difference? They all convert energy from one form to another, turning potential (stored) energy into kinetic energy (motion). But the way they do it is different, and so is the type of energy. An engine uses fuel to create heat that it converts into motion. In a car—hybrid or regular— the engine burns gasoline, a chemical reaction, to move the pistons. A motor doesn't use fuel, like gasoline, to produce motion; it uses electricity. In a hybrid car, the electricity comes from a battery, which stores the energy. A generator works like a motor in reverse. In fact, motors and generators have the same parts, and both work by rotating a wire coil in a temporary magnetic field. But instead of using electricity to create motion, like a motor, a generator uses motion to create electricity. In a hybrid car, the regenerative braking system turns the car's electric motor into a generator. During braking, the wheels turn the motor, creating electricity from the car's motion.

TRY THIS!

BLOW THE BALLAST!

MAKE A SUBMARINE DIVE AND SURFACE

Ever wonder how a submarine as long as a football field can dive under water and surface again? You can try it for yourself. You'll make a sub that works like the navy's huge boats.

WHAT YOU NEED

TIME: about an hour

Ask an adult to help.

1. 2-liter plastic bottle, empty and clean

2. Balloon

3. Clean plastic tubing, approximately 3 feet (1 m) long with a diameter between 0.4 and 0.9 inches (9.5 to 22 mm)

4. 1 to 3 table knives, depending how heavy they are

5. Electrical or duct tape

6. Electric drill

7. Bathtub, kitchen sink, or big bucket with a foot or two (30.5 to 61 cm) of water

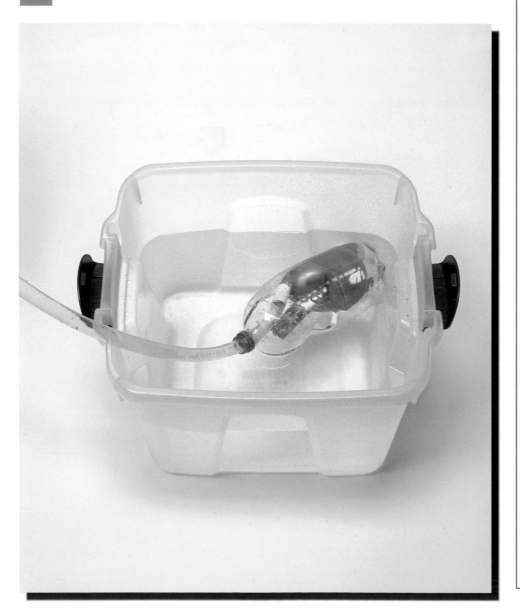

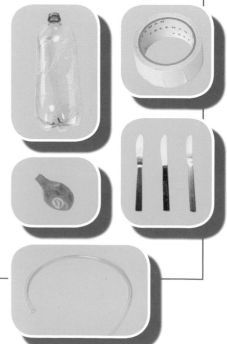

1. ASK AN ADULT TO drill four ½-inch (1.3 cm) holes in the plastic bottle. Make two holes near the top, on opposite sides, and two holes near the bottom, on opposite sides.

2. PUT THE TABLE KNIVES inside the bottle for ballast. (Ballast is weight that helps to keep a ship stable.) You only need enough knives to help your sub sink slowly. (You may want to test this step by itself in the water, but then be sure to dry the outside of the bottle.)

3. STRETCH THE BALLOON A bit so that it's easy to blow up, or inflate and deflate it a couple of times.

4. PLACE THE MOUTH OF the balloon over one end of the tubing and tape it securely.

5. PUT THE BALLOON INSIDE the bottle but let most of the tubing hang out of the bottle. Position the balloon so it has enough room to inflate inside the bottle. If needed, use tape to seal around the tube at the bottle's opening.

6. LAUNCH YOUR SUBMARINE in the water. Push it down until it fills with water and is completely submerged. You may need to squeeze the bottle a few times to get rid of air bubbles.

7. AFTER THE SUB SINKS, blow into the free end of the tubing until the balloon inflates.

A KNOT ISN'T JUST SOMETHING YOU TIE IN A ROPE. IT'S ALSO THE TERM FOR MEASURING SPEED ON THE WATER, THE NUMBER OF NAUTICAL MILES TRAVELED PER HOUR. ONE KNOT EQUALS 1.151 MILES AN HOUR (1.852 KM/H).

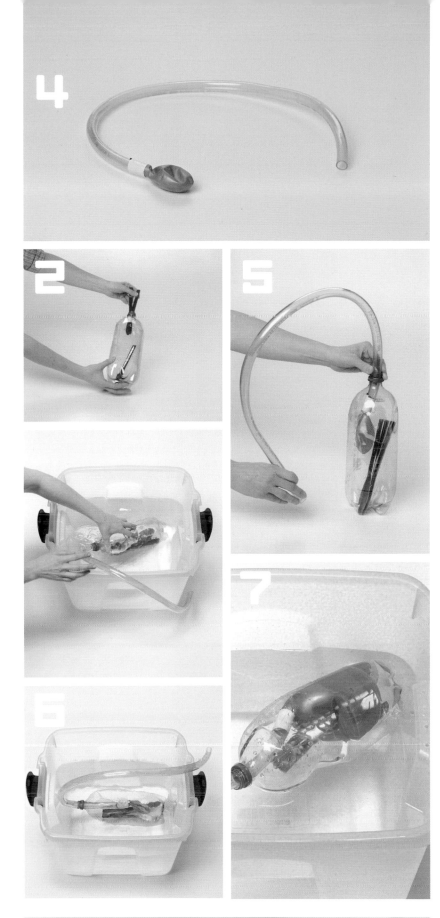

WHAT'S GOING ON?

YOUR SUBMARINE WORKS LIKE THE BALLAST TANKS ON A REAL SUBMARINE. WHEN A SUBMARINE WANTS TO DIVE, IT FLOODS ITS BALLAST TANKS WITH WATER. THE ADDITIONAL WATER MAKES THE SUB'S WEIGHT GREATER THAN THE BUOYANT FORCE THAT PUSHES IT UPWARD, AND SO THE SUB GOES DOWN. WHEN IT WANTS TO RISE TO THE SURFACE, IT FILLS ITS TANKS WITH AIR. THE AIR FORCES THE WATER OUT THROUGH VENTS (IT "BLOWS THE BALLAST"), AND THE SUB BECOMES LIGHTER. TO STAY LEVEL UNDERWATER, THE SUBMARINE BALANCES THE AMOUNT OF AIR AND WATER IN THE TANKS. CAN YOU DO THAT WITH YOUR SUB?

GLOSSARY

adhesion—an attraction holding the surfaces of two things together

air resistance—a force, created by friction, that affects things as they move through air

app—short for application, a small specialized program, or software, for a tablet, computer, smartphone, etc.

ballast—something heavy put in a vessel to help its stability

biological—related to living organisms

bionic—having artificial body parts, especially those made of electronics and mechanical devices

buoyancy—an object's ability to float

center of gravity—a point over which an object can be perfectly balanced. It's usually the same as its center of mass.

center of mass—a point that acts as though an object's mass is centered there

centrifugal force—a force that makes something that's going around a circular path move outward, away from the center of its path

cohesion—an attraction holding the particles of something together

compound machine—a machine made up of two or more simple machines

condensation—when a gas changes to a liquid

conduction—when heat or electricity moves from one place to another

convection—when heat rises and cooler air or liquid takes its place, creating a constant circular motion

drag—a force opposing something as it moves forward through air or liquid

evaporation—when a liquid changes to a gas

excitation—when a particle jumps up a level in energy, as when it's heated, and moves around more

forces of flight—the forces of lift, weight, thrust, and drag, which push or pull on an airplane or rocket in motion

frequency—the number of times a wave moves up and down in one second

friction—when two things rub against each other, creating heat

gravity—the force of attraction between any two things

hovercraft—a vehicle that glides along on a cushion of air

hydraulics—using liquid to move things

inertia—a measure of how difficult it is to change an object's state of motion—that is, to move it if it's still or change the way it's moving if it's in motion

insulator—a material that does not easily let electricity or heat or sound get through

kinetic energy—the energy of motion

laser—a concentrated beam of polarized light

lever—a simple machine consisting of a long bar that exerts a bigger force when you push or pull it

GLOSSARY

lift—a force created by an airplane or rocket so it can rise up

magnetic field—an area around a magnet, or magnetic material, where the magnets try to pull together or push apart

mass—a measure of the amount of stuff that something is made of

mechanical—using a tool or machine part, which is moved by a force

molecule—the smallest particle of something. A molecule is made of atoms held together by chemical bonds.

photoconductivity—when something absorbs light and has a change in how electrical charges flow through it

polarization—when light waves (or other things that radiate) are restricted in the way they vibrate

potential energy—stored-up energy

radiation—when energy— such as heat, light, or sound—travels outward

resistance—a force that has to be overcome for movement

resonance—the quality of a sound created by sound waves

robot—a machine that gathers information about its environment and uses it to follow instructions to do something

rolling resistance—a force, created by friction, that affects something when it rolls on a surface

screw—a simple machine made of a pointed nail with grooves running around it. The grooves act like an inclined plane, making it easier for you to drive it into wood or another material.

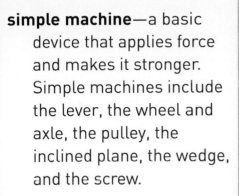

simple machine—a basic device that applies force and makes it stronger. Simple machines include the lever, the wheel and axle, the pulley, the inclined plane, the wedge, and the screw.

siphon—an upside-down U-shaped tube that moves liquid using gravity, not pumps

spectrum—the entire range of radio waves, light waves, etc.

static electricity—an electrical charge, typically made by friction

thrust—a force created by a rocket or airplane so it can move forward

tractor beam—a beam of energy that holds an object and can move it toward the beam's source

wedge—a simple machine made of something that's pointed at one end and thick at the other. You use it to focus force at its sharp point.

weight—the measure of the force of gravity on an object

wheel and axle—a simple machine consisting of a wheel rotating on a rod. It helps you move things by reducing friction and increasing force.

FIND OUT MORE!

Websites

Adventures in Chemistry
acs.org/content/acs/en/education/
whatischemistry/adventures-in-
chemistry.html
The American Chemical Society's site with lots of fun science secrets, experiments, and games.

Explain That Stuff!
explainthatstuff.com
British science writer Chris Woodford's excellent site with lots of fun, easy-to-understand articles about how things work.

NASA
nasa.gov/audience/forstudents/
index.html
Lots of spacey information, broken down by grade level.

National Geographic Kids
kids.nationalgeographic.com
Articles, videos, and games about science, nature, and all kinds of cool stuff.

Wonderopolis
wonderopolis.org/wonders
Articles about many wonders, including ones in science, technology, and math.

Inspiration for making your own musical instrument:

Bash the Trash
bashthetrash.com/Instruments_
Intro/Instruments.html

New York Philharmonic
nyphilkids.org/games/main.phtml?

Atlanta Symphony Orchestra
atlantasymphony.org/aso/
asoassets/downloadcenter/
Symphony Street Activity Sheets.pdf

Dallas Symphony Orchestra
dsokids.com/activities-at-home/
make-instrument/.aspx

Videos

"Carrot Clarinet"
Musician Linsey Pollak makes a delicious musical instrument during a demonstration for TEDx Sydney 2014.
tedxsydney.com/talk/carrot
-clarinet-linsey-pollak/

Landfill Harmonic
This documentary site has a movie trailer and interesting facts about the Recycled Orchestra of Cateura, Paraguay.
landfillharmonicmovie.com

Books

Accidental Genius: The World's Greatest By-Chance Discoveries by Richard Gaughan (Metro Books, 2010) A fun look at discoveries old and new and the scientific processes behind them, best for more advanced readers.

Hedy Lamarr by Ann Gaines (Rourke Publishing, 2002) A short biography of the famous actress and inventor, best for younger readers, from the Discover the Life of an Inventor series.

Helen Greiner: Cofounder of the iRobot Corporation by Mary Schulte (Kidhaven Press, 2009) A 48-page biography, suitable for upper elementary and middle school students, from the Innovators series.

Microwave Man: Percy Spencer and His Sizzling Invention by Sara L. Latta (Enslow Publishers, 2014) A slim biography of Percy Spencer, great for younger readers, from the Inventors at Work! series.

The Noblest Invention: An Illustrated History of the Bicycle by the editors of *Bicycling* magazine (Rodale, 2003) An interesting look at bikes and cycling for advanced readers.

Science: A Visual Encyclopedia (DK Publishers, 2014) A wide-ranging and engaging look at many areas of science, great discoveries, and scientists. Written by Chris Woodford and Steve Parker, this encyclopedia is great for 7- to 12-year-olds.

Try This! 50 Fun Experiments for the Mad Scientist in You by Karen Romano Young (National Geographic Kids, 2014) Fun hands-on science for young explorers.

INDEX

Boldface indicates illustrations.

INDEX CONT.

CREDITS

All diagrams created by Lachina unless otherwise noted below.

Just the Facts icons throughout by Sanjida Rashid.

CO = Corbis; GI = Getty Images; NGC = National Geographic Creative; SS = Shutterstock

FRONT COVER: space ship, Geoffrey Holman/GI; girl on bike, Chuck Haney/Danita Delimont.com; exoskeleton suit, John B. Carnett/Bonnier Corp./GI; roller coaster, ChameleonsEye/SS; dog, Thinkstock Images/Stockbyte/Getty Images; robot, vladru/GI; BACK COVER: satellite, NASA; All Illustrations by Lachina. SPINE: dog, Thinkstock Images/Stockbyte/GI; 2 (UP), Justin Fantl; 2 (LO), AGF/Photoshot; 3, iRobot; 7, sashahaltam/SS

CHAPTER 1
8-9, Westend61/GI; 11, Amblin/Universal/The Kobal Collection; 12 (UP), Arx Pax; 12 (LO), The Kobal Collection/Lucasfilm/20th Century Fox; 13 (LO LE), The Kobal Collection/Studio Ghibli/Tokuma Shoten; 13 (LO CTR), Amblin/Universal/The Kobal Collection; 13 (LO RT), Photos 12/Alamy; 14 (UP), Popperfoto/GI; 14 (LO LE), GIPhotoStock/Science Source; 14 (LO RT), Daily Herald Archive/SSPL/Hulton Archive Creative/GI; 15 (RT), The Advertising Archives; 17, Portra Images/Stone Sub/GI; 18 (UP), WENN.com/Newscom; 18 (LO LE), design36/SS; 18 (CTR), Uchiyama Ryu/Nature Production/Minden Pictures; 18 (LO CTR), Ensuper/SS; 18 (LO RT), Mihai Simonia/SS; 20 (LO LE), Charles D. Winters/Science Source; 20 (LO RT), 4X-image/GI; 20 (UP), Paramount Tv/The Kobal Collection/Yarish, Michae; 21 (LO), MGM/The Kobal Collection; 22 (UP), Roberto Rizzo/SS; 22 (LO LE), Alfred Eisenstaedt/Time & Life Pictures/GI; 22 (LO RT), CBS/GI; 23 (UP), nito/SS; 23 (CTR LE), U.S. Patent/Public Domain; 23 (CTR RT), Production Perig/SS; 23 (LO), AG-PHOTOS/SS; 25, Jorge Silva/Reuters; 26 (UP), U.S. Air Force/Staff Sgt. Bennie J. Davis III; 26 (LO), Mopic/SS; 27 (LO LE), University of Rochester; 27 (LO RT), University of Rochester; 28 (LO), Science Photo Library RF/GI; 28 (UP), University of Rochester; 29 (RT), Licensed By: Warner Bros. Entertainment Inc. All Rights Reserved; 31, Rick Wilking/Reuters; 33 (UP RT), John B. Carnett/Bonnier Corp./GI; 33 (LO), Kenneth Garrett/NGC; 34 (UP), Devore, Sora/NGC; 34 (LO), Allegra Boverman; 35 (LO), Allegra Boverman; 35 (UP), Allegra Boverman; 37, CBS/GI; 38-39 (LO), koya979/SS; 39 (LE),

donatas1205/SS; 39 (RT), Jono Halling; 40, Dorling Kindersley/GI; 41 (LO), CO RF/Alamy; 42-43 (ALL), Rebecca Hale, NGS

CHAPTER 2
44-45, Westend61/GI; 47, Jay P. Morgan/Photolibrary RM/GI; 48 (UP), Nina Leen/The LIFE Picture Collection/GI; 48 (CTR LE), Mega Pixel/SS; 48 (CTR RT), Everett Collection/SS; 48 (LO), March Of Time/The LIFE Picture Collection/GI; 49 (UP-Chicken), Diana Taliun/SS; 49 (UP-Takeout box), bestv/SS; 49 (UP-Cake), Semen Kuzmin/SS; 49 (UP-Tacos), julie deshaies/SS; 49 (UP-Bananas), Maks Narodenko/SS; 49 (UP-Mango), Maks Narodenko/SS; 49 (LO), Komar/SS; 50 (LO LE), Tewan Banditrukkanka/SS; 50 (LO CTR), Yuriy Dmitriev for Electrolux Design Lab; 50 (LO RT), Yuriy Dmitriev for Electrolux Design Lab; 51 (CTR LE), Jim Barber/SS; 51 (LO LE), Larsen & Talbert//Photolibrary RMGI; 51 (UP RT), Monika Nesslauer/GI; 51 (CTR RT), Monika Nesslauer/GI; 51 (LO RT), Monika Nesslauer/GI; 53, Brand New Images/Taxi/GI; 54 (UP RT), Neale Clark/Robert Harding/CO; 54 (UP LE), Maurizio Biso/Alamy; 54 (CTR LE), topimages/SS; 54 (CTR), Andrew Ilyasov/E+/GI; 54 (CTR RT), Grigorev Mikhail/SS; 54 (LO), Eric Isselee/SS; 56 (LO RT), Serhiy Kobyakov/SS; 57 (LO), AP Photo/James D. Morgan/REX; 57 (UP RT), RMN (Musèe Guimet)/Thierry Ollivier/Art Resource, NY; 59, Sergemi/SS; 60 (CTR), Michael Phillips/iStockphoto/GI; 60 (LE), SS; 61 (LO), Plasteed/SS; 62 (UP-silverware), Sukharevskyy Dmytro/SS; 62 (UP-"No" symbol), SS; 62 (LO LE), Dima Fadeev/SS; 62 (LO RT), Claudio Divizia/SS; 63 (LO RT), Kalin Eftimov/SS; 64 (UP), Roberto Rizzo/SS; 64 (LO), Paul Popper/Popperfoto/GI; 65 (LO LE), Pictorial Parade/Archive Photos/GI; 65 (UP), courtesy Raytheon Company; 65 (LO RT), courtesy LG Electronics; 67, Javier Pierini/The Image Bank/GI; 68 (UP), Andrew Lees; 68 (LO), Sebastian Kaulitz/SS; 69 (LO), Javier Brosch/SS; 70, Brad Barket/GI for WIRED/GI; 70-71, The Kobal Collection/Lucasfilm/20th Century Fox; 71 (UP), Joanne Rathe/The Boston Globe/GI; 71 (CTR), AP Photo; 71 (LO RT), iRobot; 71 (LO LE), AP Photo/Mohammad al Sehety; 73, Andersen Ross/Stockbyte/GI; 74 (UP), SPK/Alamy; 74 (LO LE), courtesy Herbeau Creations of America; 74 (LO CTR), JemalWright.com; 74 (LO RT), JemalWright.com; 75 (LO), Yoshikazu Tsuno/AFP/GI; 76 (UP), ChinaFotoPress/

UPPA/UPPA/ZUMAPRESS/Newscom; 76 (LO LE), Andrey_Kuzmin/SS; 76 (LO RT), 3Dsculptor/SS; 77 (LO), Tom Nick Cocotos; 78-79 (ALL), Rebecca Hale, NGS

CHAPTER 3
80-81, Westend61/GI; 83, Kisialiou Yury/SS; 84 (UP), Copyright SMART Technologies. All rights reserved.; 84 (LO LE), AS400 DB/CO; 84 (LO RT), Stephen C. Dickson/Creative Commons (https://creativecommons.org/licenses/by-sa/4.0/legalcode); 85 (lo A), J. R. Eyerman/The LIFE Picture Collection/GI; 85 (lo B), PhotoAlto/Alamy; 85 (lo C), aber-CPC/Alamy; 85 (lo D), Prasit Rodphan/SS; 85 (lo E), AP Photo/Franka Bruns; 86 (LE), PathDoc/SS; 86 (CTR), Thomas Bethge/SS; 86 (RT), Kenishirotie/SS; 87 (RT), Sickles Photo-Reporting Service/GI; 89, Rebecca Hale, NGS, 90 (LE), Mega Pixel/SS; 90 (CTR), Mega Pixel/SS; 90 (RT), Stan Munro/Caters News/Newscom; 91 (UP RT), Warner Bros/The Kobal Collection; 91 (LO RT), Bob Ingelhart/E+/GI; 92 (LO LE), Zygotehaasnobrain/SS; 92 (LO RT), xtock/SS; 92 (UP), Roberto Rizzo/SS; 93 (UP LE), Zygotehaasnobrain/SS; 93 (UP RT), Monika Gniot/SS; 93 (CTR RT), Julia Sudnitskaya/SS; 93 (LO RT), SS, 93 (LO LE), Shannon Stapleton/Reuters/CO; 95, 4x6/E+/GI; 96 (UP LE), Ensuper/SS; 96 (LO), rangizzz/SS; 96 (UP RT), Studio Barcelona/SS; 97 (RT), dustin steller/E+/GI; 98 (UP), marinini/SS; 98 (LO LE), Petr Malyshev/SS; 98 (LO RT), Katie Smith Photography/SS; 99 (LO), Everett Collection Historical/Alamy; 101, Jean-Michel Labat/ardea.com/Pantheon/SuperStock; 102 (UP), Ted Kinsman/Science Source; 102 (CTR), alisafarov/SS; 102 (LO), Mouse in the House/Alamy; 103 (LO), National Galleries Of Scotland/GI; 105, Chris Price/E+/GI; 106 (UP), Splash News/Newscom; 106 (CTR), AP Photo/Rex Features; 106 (LO), Nicolas Primola/SS; 107 (CTR LE), Vereshchagin Dmit/SS; 107 (CTR RT), pbombaert/SS; 107 (LO), Vereshchagin Dmit/SS; 108 (LO LE), Hero Images Inc/Alamy; 108 (LO RT), Eric Isselee/SS; 108 (CTR), Joe Ravi/SS; 108 (UP), Vereshchagin Dmit/SS; 109, Iaroslav Neliubov/SS; 109 (LO RT), Kamil Macniak/SS; 109 (UP), Vereshchagin Dmit/SS; 109 (CTR LE), Vereshchagin Dmit/SS; 109 (LO CTR), Vereshchagin Dmit/SS; 109 (LO LE), Vereshchagin Dmit/SS; 109 (LO RT), pbombaert/SS; 110, courtesy Landfill Harmonic; 111 (UP), epa european pressphoto agency b.v./Alamy; 111 (CTR), courtesy Landfill Harmonic; 111 (LO LE), courtesy Landfill Harmonic; 111 (LO RT), courtesy Landfill

Harmonic; 113, kenny hung photography/ Flickr Open/GI; 114 (UP), ogwen/SS; 114 (CTR), Chak/SS; 114 (LO-Globe), adike/SS; 114 (LO-pencils), SS; 115 (LO LE), Louella938/SS; 115 (LO CTR), Lyudmila Suvorova/SS; 115 (LO RT), Nick Barounis/SS; 116 (LO LE), v.s.anandhakrishna/SS; 116 (LO RT), igor.stevanovic/SS; 116 (CTR), Kostsov/ SS; 116 (UP), Chak/SS; 117 (UP RT), Rebecca Hale, NGS; 117 (LO), Giakita/Alamy; 118-119 (ALL), Rebecca Hale, NGS

CHAPTER 4
120-121, Westend61/GI; 123, ChameleonsEye/SS; 125 (LE), Noah K. Murray/The Star-Ledger/CO; 125 (RT), Henry Lee/China Photo/GI; 126 (UP), Chris Batson/ Alamy; 126 (LO RT), Marie Hansen/The LIFE Picture Collection/GI; 126 (LO LE), Sergej Razvodovskij/SS; 127 (RT), Florilegius/Alamy; 128 (UP), Roberto Rizzo/SS; 128 (LO), Rob Crandall/Alamy; 128-9, Richard Cummins/ CO; 129 (UP), Joshua Sudock/The Orange County Register/Zuma Press; 129 (LO), Randy Risling/Toronto Star/GI; 131, Lucy Nicholson/ Reuters; 132 (UP), epa european pressphoto agency b.v./Alamy; 132 (CTR), iStock/GI; 132 (LO), David Peeters/iStockphoto/GI; 133 (LO LE), iStock/GI; 134 (UP), Jorge Salcedo/SS; 134 (CTR), focal point/SS; 134 (LO LE), Everett Historical/SS; 134 (LO RT), Michael Ochs Archives/GI; 135 (LO), Philip Gendreau/CO; 137, Thinkstock Images/Stockbyte/GI; 138

(UP), imageBROKER/Alamy; 138 (CTR RT), Agencja Fotograficzna Caro/Alamy; 138 (CTR LE), Norbert Michalke/F1online RM/ GI; 138 (LO), NASA; 139 (LO LE), ssuaphotos/SS; 139 (LO RT), Zoran Radmanovic/SS; 140 (LE), Siloto/Alamy; 140 (RT), Juffin/GI; 141 (LO RT), Pitchal/Sygma/CO; 142, Bettmann/CO; 143 (LO), U.S. Patent/Public Domain; 143 (CTR), Roberson Museum and Science Center, Binghamton, New York; 143 (UP), U.S. Patent/Public Domain; 145, Simon Bottomley/Photographer's Choice RF/GI; 146, Nils Jorgensen/REX/Newscom; 148 (RT), David McNew/GI; 148 (LE), Picsfive/SS; 149 (LO RT), Image Source/CO; 149 (LO LE), Monkey Business Images/SS; 151, Beatriz Pitarch/Flickr RF/GI; 152 (ctr A), Jean-Marc Giboux/AP Images for Discovery Communications; 152 (ctr B), Brian Hickey/Alamy; 152 (ctr C), Hulton Archive/GI; 152 (ctr D), CUTRARO/AFP/GI; 152 (ctr E), Amy Harris/Dreamstime.com; 152 (ctr F), johavel/SS; 152 (LE), Matej Kastelic/SS; 152 (LO RT), LOOK Die Bildagentur der Fotografen GmbH/Alamy; 153 (RT), Mary Evans Picture Library; 154-155 (ALL), Rebecca Hale, NGS

CHAPTER 5
156-157, Westend61/GI; 159, Blend Images/ Alamy; 160 (UP), Library of Congress Prints and Photographs Division, #04039; 160 (lo A), William Perugini/SS; 160 (lo B),

Protasov AN/SS; 160 (lo E), Aleksandrs Tihonovs/Alamy; 160 (lo C), Aija Lehtonen/ SS.com; 160 (lo D), Miguel Medina/AFP/GI; 161 (LO), AP Photo/REX/Varibike/Solent News; 162 (CTR), courtesy Spruzza; 162 (LO), Goddard New Era/Alamy; 163 (RT), Lori Adamski Peek/Riser/GI; 164 (UP LE), Roberto Rizzo/SS; 164 (le A), Leemage/CO; 164 (CTR), AS400 DB/CO; 164 (le B), Prisma/UIG/GI; 164 (le C), Wallace G. Levison/The LIFE Picture Collection/GI; 164 (ri A), Rischgitz/Hulton Archive/GI; 164 (ri B), Universal History Archive/GI; 164 (rt C), H. Armstrong Roberts/CO; 164 (rt D), Muzaffer Akarca/E+/GI; 165 (UP LE), Hulton Archiv/GI; 165 (LO LE), Old Paper Studios/ Alamy; 165 (UP RT), Matt McClain/The Washington Post/GI—photographed from Waterview Condominium; 165 (LO RT), Thailand Travel and Stock/SS; 167, EPA/Uli Deck/CO; 168 (CTR), Kiyoshi Ota/ Bloomberg/GI; 168 (LO), Library of Congress Prints and Photographs Division, #10400; 169 (LO RT), Tupungato/SS; 170 (LO RT), WENN.com/Newscom; 171 (LO RT), Oxford Science Archive/Print Collector/GI; 173, Rob Whitworth/Photolibrary RM/GI; 174 (UP RT), courtesy of author; 174 (UP RT), Norman Barrett/Alamy; 174 (LE), Box912/SS; 175 (RT), ChinaFotoPress/GI; 177, age fotostock/Alamy; 178 (UP), Everett Historical/SS; 178 (CTR LE), Vukicevic/ Panoramic/ZUMAPRESS/Newscom; 178 (CTR RT), Paul Nicklen /NGC; 178 (LO CTR), Mark Thiessen/NGC; 178 (LO RT), Rémi Kaupp/Creative Commons; 178 (CTR CTR), SS; 179 (RT), SSPL/GI; 180 (LO), The Art Archive/Musée Carnavalet Paris/Dagli Orti; 181 (CTR LE), violetkaipa/SS; 181 (CTR RT), Flynt/Dreamstime.com; 183, Catherine MacBride/Flickr RM/GI; 184 (UP), David Ducros/Science Source; 184, NASA; 185 (lo A), GI/Dorling Kindersley RF/SuperStock; 185 (lo B), NASA/Goddard Space Flight Center; 185 (lo C), U.S. Air Force/NGC/CO; 185 (lo D), Sovfoto/UIG via GI; 185 (lo E, F, G, H, I), NASA; 186 (UP), Taylor Hill/GC Images/GI; 187 (UP), Dan Tuffs/GI; 187 (LO RT), Tesla Motors/EyePress/Newscom; 187 (LO LE), Marvel Enterprises/The Kobal Collection; 189, Imgorthand/F+/GI; 190 (UP), Car Culture/CO; 190 (LO LE), NASA Langley/David C. Bowman; 190 (LO CTR), FlugKerl2/Creative Commons (https://creativecommons.org/licenses/by-sa/3.0/ legalcode); 190 (LO RT), Nick Saffell/ University of Cambridge; 190, NASA; 192 (RT), Teddy Leung/SS; 192 (LE), Anthony Collins Cycling/Alamy; 194-195 (ALL), Rebecca Hale, NGS; 199 (UP), Allegra Boverman; 199 (LO), Jean-Michel Labat/ ardea.com/Pantheon/SuperStock; 200, Joshua Sudock/The Orange County Register/Zuma Press; 201 (UP), koya979/ SS; 201 (LO), Komar/SS; 202, Javier Brosch/ SS; 203, Portra Images/Stone Sub/GI; 208, Thinkstock Images/Stockbyte/GI

For Connor and Ryan, who never hesitate to tackle the impossible. —TJR

Thanks to Shelby Alinsky for her vision, guidance, and good humor; Santiago Casares, Katharine Manning, David McMullin, and Shelley Walden for their insight and fellowship; and Jim Monke for his unflagging support.

The publisher also wishes to thank Paul Stysley of NASA and David Grier of NYU, and the book team: Shelby Alinsky, Kathryn Williams, Julide Dengel, Lori Epstein, Michelle Harris, Joan Gossett, and Rachel Kenny.

Julide Dengel, *Art Director/Designer*
Simon Reinwick, *Designer*

Since 1888, the National Geographic Society has funded more than 12,000 research, exploration, and preservation projects around the world. The Society receives funds from National Geographic Partners LLC, funded in part by your purchase. A portion of the proceeds from this book supports this vital work.

For more information, please visit nationalgeographic.com, call 1-800-647-5463, or write to the following address:
National Geographic Partners
1145 17th Street N.W.
Washington, D.C. 20036-4688 U.S.A.

Visit us online at nationalgeographic.com/books

For librarians and teachers: ngchildrensbooks.org

More for kids from National Geographic:
kids.nationalgeographic.com

For information about special discounts for bulk purchases, please contact National Geographic Books Special Sales: ngspecsales@ngs.org

For rights or permissions inquiries, please contact National Geographic Books Subsidiary Rights: ngbookrights@ngs.org

Trade edition ISBN: 978-1-4263-2555-7
Reinforced library edition ISBN: 978-1-4263-2556-4

Printed in Hong Kong
16/THK/1